T0106516

AuthorHouse™
1663 Liberty Drive
Bloomington, IN 47403
www.authorhouse.com
Phone: 1-800-839-8640

Published by AuthorHouse   03/29/2012

ISBN: 978-1-4685-6096-1 (sc)
ISBN: 978-1-4685-6094-7 (e)

Library of Congress Control Number: 2012904300

Any people depicted in stock imagery provided by Thinkstock are models, and such images are being used for illustrative purposes only. Certain stock imagery © Thinkstock.

This book is printed on acid-free paper.

Because of the dynamic nature of the Internet, any web addresses or links contained in this book may have changed since publication and may no longer be valid. The views expressed in this work are solely those of the author and do not necessarily reflect the views of the publisher, and the publisher hereby disclaims any responsibility for them.

The storm picture with rotating clouds in the front cover was taken by James G. Ladue when a large tornado was developing near him.

**The 1925 Tri-State Tornado's Devastation in Franklin County,
Hamilton County, and White County, Illinois**

———∾∾◦⊙◦∾∾———

This story shows where this devastating tornado hit many homes, buildings, and farms as it crossed these counties and tells what many local people experienced and who was killed.

———∾∾◦⊙◦∾∾———

Six Mile Township

From south of Royalton to southeast of Zeigler

As the tornado was rapidly approaching Franklin County, several students at Royalton Grade School on the southwestern side of town could see what to them looked like a big, black mass. As it was about to enter Six Mile Township, they could see it was passing by to the south of them. The tornado was three-quarters to one mile wide as it was entering Franklin County. As the northern edge of the tornado got into Six Mile Township, it badly damaged several homes in the "Hub Town" area just south of Royalton. Then, as the rest of the tornado got into Six Mile Township, complete destruction was occurring.

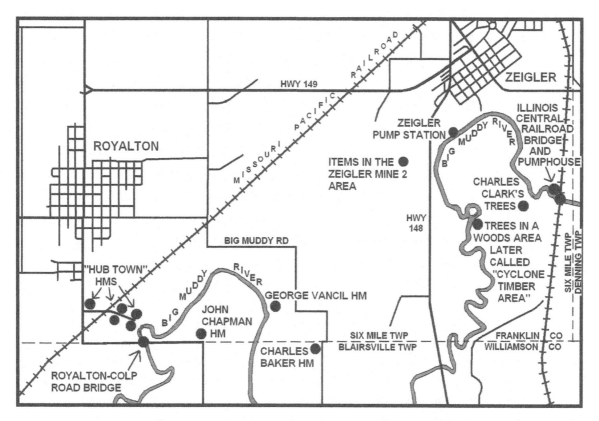

Black circle points that show tornado damage locations next to the Franklin-Williamson County line and in south central and southeast SixMile Township. On this and the rest of the Franklin County damage location maps, more recent roads and what they are called are shown so you can tell where the 1925 tornado damage occurred. Also, a few of the roads that were there in 1925 and had been taken away sometime later, have been placed on these maps.

In the 1920s, the main road between Royalton and Colp crossed Big Muddy River along the county line just south of the Royalton waterworks area. This is where the first complete destruction occurred in Six Mile Township since the Royalton-Colp big iron road bridge was completely blown away.

3

A half-mile farther east, just on the northern side of the county line, was John and Lillian Chapman's home. When Lillian saw the tornado approaching, she quickly took her two young daughters, Irene and Dorothy, outside and got into a ditch. As the tornado arrived, their home was completely destroyed, and Lillian was severely injured when a two-by-four piece of wood was blown into her side. Her husband, John, was working in a mine near Royalton. When he started home on his horse after the tornado had occurred, he and his horse had to swim across Big Muddy River since the bridge had been destroyed. When he got home, he found that Lillian had been badly injured, so he took her to the hospital in Herrin. Unfortunately, she died twelve days later on March 30. She was the first person to be severely injured in Franklin County.

Shown on the county line south of Royalton is where a part of the Royalton-Colp Road Bridge over the Big Muddy River was destroyed by the tornado. (Photo courtesy of Lynda Savka)

Just around the Chapman's house was what then was called Vancil Bend of Big Muddy River. On the eastern side of the bend and the eastern side of the river was George Vancil's home. George was building a new home nearby but had not yet finished it. He, his wife, Versie, their children, Carl and Violet, and two babies were in their home when the tornado came through. Both the old and new homes were completely destroyed. George was severely injured when a two-by-four piece of wood was blown through his chest and he died soon afterward. Versie and Carl were injured with cuts on their heads. Versie was blown away from the house area while she was holding her two babies. Although Versie was badly injured, her babies were not hurt much. Violet's leg was broken, and she landed under debris.

George and Versie's two oldest children, Vivian and Vernon, had been at school that day in Blairsville Township, Williamson County. As they were walking home from school that afternoon, they saw the storm coming toward them, so they stopped at Charlie and Mary Baker's home near the county line. The Bakers took them down into their cellar just before the tornado arrived, and all of them were able to keep from getting hurt. The Baker's home was blown off its foundation and damaged. However, it was not destroyed.

As the tornado continued to rapidly move across Six Mile Township, many of the high school students in Zeigler could see the tornado moving along the township and passing south of them. They were able to easily see it since the high school's second floor had large windows on the southern side of the building. As student Rachel Whiteside saw the tornado moving along the township, to her, it looked like dark clouds rolling around on the ground with pieces of debris flying into the air. It sounded like a train was going by.

After the tornado first roared into Six Mile Township and completely destroyed the homes of John Chapman and George Vancil, very few other homes were known to have been completely destroyed across the rest of the township. The area where the tornado moved across was near a part of the Big Muddy River where there were forested areas and not many homes and people in this part of the township. Much of the severe damage in this area was to the trees. The tree damage in this region was noticeable for many years, and because of this, one of the forest areas near the river, about a mile south of Zeigler, was called "Cyclone Timber Area."

Besides the damage to trees in this area, there was some damage to buildings and other things. Up near the northern edge of the tornado damage path just south of Zeigler, some minor damage was done to some items in the Zeigler Mine #2 area and the Zeigler pump station next to Big Muddy River. Also, as the tornado reached the eastern edge of Six Mile Township, it crossed the Illinois Central Railroad and caused some very severe damage in the area where the railroad crossed Big Muddy River. The tornado shifted the railroad bridge, one-eighth of a mile long, several feet off its foundation pillars. Near the bridge, the Illinois Central Railroad pump house and water tower were completely destroyed.

As the tornado roared across Six Mile Township, two people died as the tornado hit them. Fortunately, because the tornado moved mostly along and near Big Muddy River in this township, where there were forests, few homes, and not as many people as elsewhere, no more people in this township died because of the tornado.

Denning Township

From the Plumfield area to the northern part of West Frankfort

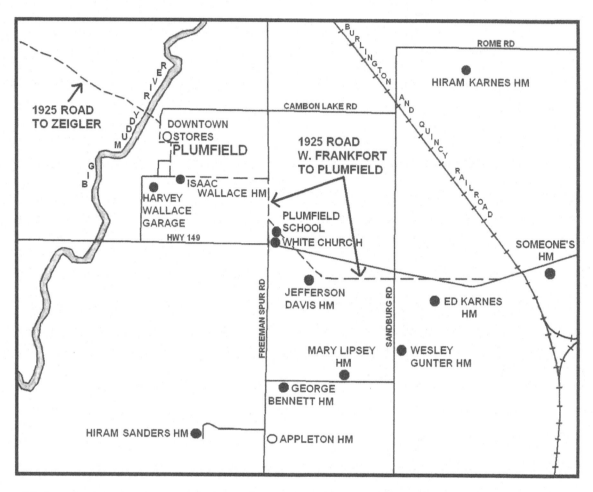

Black circle points that show tornado damage locations in southwest Denning Township and part of Plumfield. Two white circle points show where things were not hit by the tornado and were not damaged.

As the tornado moved into Denning Township, it was almost a mile wide and began to affect areas east of Big Muddy River, where many more people lived. It passed south of downtown Plumfield, so none of the stores were known to have been damaged. South of the store area, Harvey Wallace's wooden garage was blown away. His father, Isaac Wallace, had a nearby home that was slightly damaged.

However, farther southeast, there was complete destruction. The White Church and Plumfield School were about a half-mile southeast of downtown Plumfield and well in the path of the tornado. Isaac's twelve-year-old daughter, Nellie, was at school at the time, along with many other students, including Barbara Hamon, Anna Johnson, and Eva Johnson. To Nellie, the tornado looked like a big, black cloud, and she thought there would be just heavy rain rather than a tornado. Sarah Davis, who was at the Ladies Aid meeting in nearby White Church, saw the storm coming and knew it was dangerous. She rushed to the school before the tornado arrived and held on to Nellie. Then the tornado hit and completely destroyed White Church and Plumfield School. The only thing left of the two-room school was the floor. Both Sarah and Nellie were blown out and into the school ground. Nellie was able to hold on to a two-foot-high tree to keep from being blown farther away, and she was not badly injured. However, Sarah was badly injured when some large tree limbs fell onto her, and she died several days later. Black mud covered Nellie. Later, when her father, Isaac, and brother, Harvey, drove toward the school and looked for her, they did not recognize the muddy person they saw as her.

Several other students, including Eva Johnson, were trapped when a wall of one side of the school building fell on them. Some big schoolboys were able to pull the wall off them, and Eva was able to get out. Getting out quickly was important because the school stove had started a fire in the debris of the building.

Unfortunately, students Barbara Hamon and Anna Johnson were killed when the school was destroyed. Many other students were injured, including Eva Johnson. When the school was rebuilt after this event occurred, a very large storm cellar was also built so teachers and students would have a safe place to go if another tornado threatened them.

The Plumfield School before it was hit by the tornado. (Photo courtesy of Pat Hindman)

The Plumfield School after it was destroyed by the tornado. (Photo courtesy of Pat Hindman)

This large storm cellar that was built for the Plumfield School after the tornado occurred was still there when this picture was taken in April of 2007. (Photo taken by Bob Johns)

While Sarah Davis had gone to the school when the tornado was approaching, her husband, Jefferson Davis, was on their farm just southeast of the school. When the tornado arrived, Jefferson was killed instantly. The Davis's farm home was completely destroyed.

About one mile south of downtown Plumfield was Hiram and Clara Sanders's home. Several of Clara's children were home that day because they had the flu, and her younger daughter, five-year-old Reba, was there as well. As the storm was approaching from the west, Clara took her children out to the front porch on the eastern side of their home.

While they were out on the porch, Clara looked east and yelled, "Look there! Look there!"

On the Appleton's field east of them, the wind had picked up a cow, and it was being blown over toward their place. It landed in a field near them but was picked up again and blown past their home. Part of the western side of their home was torn off, and many of the close trees were damaged or blown down. However, none of the family members were hurt while they held on to each other on the front porch floor. The most destructive part of the almost one-mile-wide tornado passed north of them, and they were lucky they were only on the edge of the damage path. The Appleton's cow was blown away, but their home and barn were far enough south that the tornado did not damage them.

*"Reba Sanders" Bennett standing on a yard in August of 2007. She is next to where she
was in her family's home when it was damaged by the tornado back in 1925.
(Photo courtesy of "Reba Sanders" Bennett, and taken by Bob Johns)*

About a half-mile northeast of Hiram and Clara Sanders's home lived their older daughter, Naomi, and her husband, George Bennett. The Bennett's home was far enough in the tornado path that it was completely flattened with the debris being blown west into a wooded area across Freeman Spur Road. Fortunately, Naomi and George were not home when the tornado occurred.

About a half-mile east-northeast of the Bennett's home was Mary Lipsey's farm. Mary was in her home when the tornado was approaching, and she got into her storm cellar with some relatives who were visiting her. Her barn was completely destroyed, but her rather large home was only damaged and moved around on its foundation.

East-northeast of Mary's farm and about one mile southeast of Plumfield School was Wesley Gunter Sr.'s home. The tornado completely destroyed this home. Several family members were injured, and the baby, Wesley Gunter Jr., was killed.

Just northeast of the Gunter's home, the tornado also destroyed Ed Karnes's home. Fortunately, no one was killed there. Ed saw the storm coming, and he and his wife quickly got into their storm cellar, which they had built after a tornado in 1912 came through the area and scared them.

Hiram Karnes, who was Ed's brother, had a home almost a mile north of Ed's home. As the tornado was approaching, Hiram's wife, Lillie, took their children down to the cellar. Standing near the cellar door, she was able to see Hiram coming home with his horse and wagon. He was west-northwest of his home and about to turn east on Rome Road. Then the tornado came through, and because their home was near the northern edge of the tornado, it was only slightly damaged, with most of the windows blown out and some of the roof damaged. Debris was blown all around the house. Fortunately, because Hiram was north of the tornado path, he was not injured. However, the wind was so strong that his wagon was blown off the road.

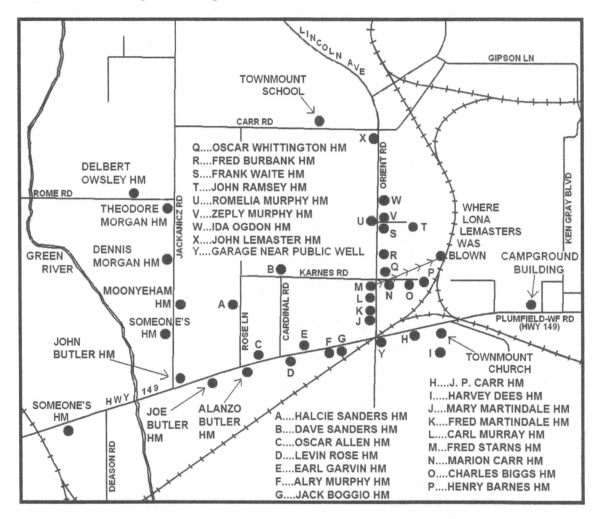

Black circle points that show tornado damage locations in the middle of Denning Township, and just west of West Frankfort. A line from one black circle point to another black circle point shows where a lady got blown away from, and where she landed.

As the nearly one-mile-wide tornado moved into central Denning Township, many more people were in danger. Several were driving their cars along Plumfield-West Frankfort Road. One was James Mason. When the tornado hit him, his car was blown off the road, and he was killed. Several cars were blown into the blown-down trees north of the road near Green River. One of these might have been James's car.

Along Jackanicz Road, several homes were destroyed, including Elbert Dennis Morgan's farm home and the nearby farm home of his son, Theodore Morgan. However, none of the Morgans were hurt since they got into their storm cellars before the tornado destroyed their homes. Similar to Ed Karnes, the Morgans had also built their storm cellars after the 1912 tornado came through the area.

Farther east, on Rose Lane, was Halcie Sanders's chicken farm. As the tornado was approaching, Halcie was not at home, but his wife, Minnie, was. She looked out the window when she heard the tornado. To her, the tornado did not look funnel cloud-shaped. Instead, it looked like fog that was rapidly rolling around a huge storm on the ground.

Zeph Murphy, who had been driving west along Plumfield-West Frankfort Road, also saw it and realized it was a large tornado. He quickly turned north onto Rose Lane and stopped at Halcie's home. He knew Halcie was at work, but he expected that Minnie was at home. He ran into the house and found that Minnie was there. When Minnie saw him, she said "I am really worried about this bad looking storm I am seeing outside". Zeph said "It is a tornado coming towards us and we need to get out of the house and get into a ditch". So they both went outside and got into a ditch. However, after thinking a bit, Minnie got back up and quickly went into her house to get her diamond rings. Unfortunately, the tornado arrived while she was still in the house, and her home was completely destroyed and blown away. The only things from the home that were not blown off the yard were an old pistol and a big heating stove. Minnie was blown onto the ground and badly injured with a large wound on one of her arms. Some neighbors came over to look for her and found her. She had so much black dirt on her body that, when they found her, they initially were not sure that it was Minnie. Zeph Murphy lost his right ear. Minnie was so badly hurt that she was taken to Barnes Hospital in Saint Louis. She almost died but, fortunately, finally got better. Well after the tornado occurred, Halcie and Minnie found that some of their paper items had been blown all the way into Indiana.

Halcie's parents, Dave and Jane Sanders, lived on Karnes Road about a quarter-mile northeast of Halcie's home. Jane's aunt, Elizabeth "Lizzie" Howard, also lived with them. Immediately after Halcie's home was destroyed, his parents' home was also demolished. Jane and Lizzie were killed instantly. Dave was badly injured and died several weeks later.

"Minnie Sanders" shown before she was badly injured by the tornado. (Photo courtesy of Dave Sanders).

Along the Plumfield-West Frankfort Road, all the way from the Plumfield School to the church campground, almost all of the homes and buildings were damaged or destroyed. As was mentioned before, both Jefferson Davis's home and Ed Karnes's home, which were near the road, were completely destroyed. Just past the Jackanicz Road, John Butler's home was damaged but not demolished. Also on John Butler's property was the home of his son, Joe Butler. Unfortunately, Joe's home was completely destroyed, and his wife, Pearl, was killed. Alanzo Butler, another son of John Butler, had a home a little farther east along the road. It was badly damaged, and its roof was blown off.

Farther east on the road, closer to the Orient Road intersection, was Arlie Murphy's home. It was completely destroyed and blown away, with the floor of the home landing on the road. For the rest of the day, and possibly longer, rescue workers and others driving on Plumfield-West Frankfort Road had to drive over Arlie's floor and other debris from the home. Fortunately, Arlie, his wife, Lois, and their children were not home when it was destroyed, so none was injured. They would find out later that one of Arlie's checks that he had in the house was blown two-hundred-and-fifty miles away to Muncie, Indiana. Also, across the road for where his house once was, Arlie found a rooster's beak had been blown into a damaged oak tree.

Still farther east on the road, past the Orient Road intersection, on a hill lived Lois's parents, J.P. and Bertha Carr. On the day of the tornado, Bertha was having a Ladies Aid meeting at her home. Lois was there, too. Everyone was in the home when the tornado was approaching. Bertha decided to go into her kitchen to close a window when the winds started getting strong. When she got into the kitchen, it was completely blown off the house, and she was injured. Fortunately, the rest of the house was only damaged but not destroyed. The other Ladies Aid people were not injured.

Farther down Plumfield-West Frankfort Road, Townmount Church was flattened, and many of its pews were blown away. To the south of the church, Harvey Dee's home was completely destroyed. The last location on the road where the tornado caused damage was in the church campground area. During the afternoon of that day, Elmer and Naomi Wallace left Plumfield to take their son, Jimmy, to see a doctor in West Frankfort. Elmer was driving the car east on the Plumfield-West Frankfort Road. After they had passed the Orient Road intersection, they realized a devastating storm coming rapidly from behind them was about to hit them. Elmer stopped their car at the church campground, and they quickly lay down in a ditch. When the tornado came through, it blew their car to the northern side of the church campground and destroyed the buildings on the campground. Fortunately, by lying in the ditch, Elmer, Naomi, and Jimmy were not injured.

The Townmount Church destroyed by the tornado. (Photo courtesy of Dave Sanders)

Arlie Murphy's six-year-old daughter, Madge, was visiting with her aunt in West Frankfort on the day the tornado occurred. Fortunately, the tornado passed well north of her aunt's home, so it was not damaged. Once her aunt heard about the storm destruction west of town, she got into her car and took Madge with her to go out and see if their family members were all right. As they drove west on Plumfield-West Frankfort Road, there was damage on the northern side of the road as they passed the Joiner School area, but not on the road. However, they had to stop near the church campground because several large oak trees had been blown down and were blocking the road. They left the car on the road and walked west along the road. Fortunately, they found that none of their family members had been killed.

"Madge Murphy" Presley in her home in November of 2006. In 1925 she was lucky to be out of her family's home
(Arlie Murphy home) since it was completely destroyed and blown out onto the road.
(Photo courtesy of "Madge Murphy" Presley, and taken by Bob Johns)

The Orient Mine #2 Office damaged by the tornado.
(Photo courtesy of the Frankfort Area Genealogy Society)

An Orient Mine #2 building west of the Office that was almost destroyed by the tornado.
(Photo courtesy of the Frankfort Area Genealogy Society)

*A place in the Orient Mine #2 area where a railroad car was blown down on five of the mine
worker's cars by the tornado. (Photo courtesy of the Frankfort Area Genealogy Society)*

*Where the tornado did damage and destruction along part of Washington Boulevard in West Frankfort.
Well to the north of the damage along this boulevard is where the Orient Mine #2 shafts can be seen
that were damaged, but not destroyed. (Photo courtesy of the Frankfort Area Genealogy Society)*

This picture that was taken up on top of one of the Orient Mine #2 shafts shows where the tornado caused much damage and destruction in West Frankfort southwest of the shaft.
(Photo courtesy of the Frankfort Area Genealogy Society)

This picture that was taken up on top of one of the Orient Mine #2 shafts shows where the tornado caused much damage and destruction in West Frankfort south of the shaft.
(Photo courtesy of the Frankfort Area Genealogy Society)

*This picture that was taken up on top of one of the Orient Mine #2 shafts shows where the tornado
caused much damage and destruction in West Frankfort southeast of the shaft.
(Photo courtesy of the Frankfort Area Genealogy Society)*

Before the tornado roared into West Frankfort, twenty-three people in Denning Township had already been killed instantly or severely injured and died later.

As the tornado devastated the northwestern part of West Frankfort in Denning Township, at least seventy more people were either killed instantly or severely injured and died later. One of the first places in West Frankfort where someone was killed instantly was in the Joiner School area, which was on the western edge of town.

Because of the large increase in students during the 1920s, two wooden-frame school buildings were constructed just north and northeast of the brick Joiner School. The first school building northeast of Joiner School was for second-grade students, and the one farther north was for first-grade students. As the tornado came through, the first-grade school building collapsed, and Charles Church's stepdaughter was killed. The second-grade school building was blown off its foundation and damaged. Fortunately, the brick Joiner School was only slightly damaged with some of its windows blown out. The first- and second-grade students were moved to the Joiner School after the tornado event.

Three of the students who were in the frame buildings on that day were Paul Ramsey, Burl Worshman, and Edward Vene. Paul had gone out of the second-grade school buildings as the tornado was approaching. He was blown into a drainage ditch but not hurt. He looked across North Illinois Street and saw a roof being blown off a house. His father, John Ramsey, later told him that their home southeast of Denning Cemetery had been completely destroyed. Fortunately, no one was there when the tornado came through.

Edward Vene was in one of the frame buildings as the tornado was approaching. The building started shaking and wobbling, and the teacher tried to get the students to lie down on the floor. However, Edward jumped out of a window and ran toward the ditch. Fortunately, he was not hurt. However, he later found out that his family's home, which was up on West Ninth Street near the two Orient Mine #2 shafts, was completely destroyed. Unfortunately, his mother, Josephine, and his brother, Albert, were in their home when it was destroyed, and they were badly injured. Josephine was never able to walk again.

Fred and Helen Worsham's son, Burl, was in the first-grade school building on that day. However, he left the school and went home well before the tornado arrived. His family's home was just southeast of the North Washington Boulevard-West Fourth Street intersection. When he got home, his mother, Helen, sent him up a block north to the Spontack grocery store to get something for her. When he started back home, the winds got very strong as the tornado was approaching, and he was blown into a red picket fence next to a neighbor's home just north of his family's home. The fence had fallen down, and he was on top of it. He looked up and could see boards and timbers flying through the sky. Then he was blown farther toward the house. A man from the house ran outside, picked up Burl, and quickly took him to the basement, where he already had his own family members. While they were in the basement, they could hear the house coming apart and glass breaking. It was damaged but not destroyed. After the tornado moved away, Burl was able to leave the neighbor's home and go to his home. He saw that it was not destroyed, but it had been blown around on its foundation. Inside, his mother's new Perfection oil stove had been blown out of the kitchen into the dining room. Burl was surprised that, from near his home, he was able to look up north and see the Orient Mine #2 shafts. Many of the homes, buildings, and trees north of where he lived had been blown down. The Spontack grocery store was damaged but still standing and not destroyed. Burl's parents were not home after the tornado occurred, so he went to his grandmother Nellie Worsham's home on North Horn Street. Her home was not damaged much because it was near the southern edge of the tornado path, but it did have almost all of its windows blown out.

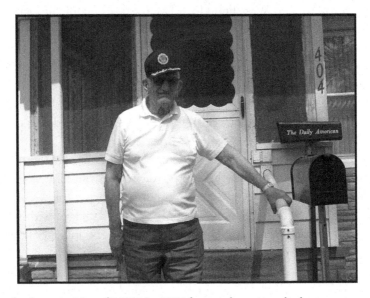

Edward Vene next to his home in May of 2007. In 1925 he was down in a ditch next to one of Joiner frame school buildings as the tornado passed over him. (Photo courtesy of Edward Vene, and taken by Bob Johns)

*Burl Worsham standing next to a house in May of 2007 that used to be the Spontack Store that he had gone to get
something for his mother before he started back home, and got blown over by strong winds as the tornado
was about to hit where he was in 1925. (Photo courtesy of Burl Worsham, and taken by Bob Johns)*

Several places south of the tornado path in West Frankfort had some damage because of strong
southerly winds that occurred as the tornado was going nearby. On the southern side of North Road
and west of South Taft Street, the home of neighbors of the Golio family lost part of its roof when
the strong southerly winds occurred. Pieces of the roof were blown across both North Road and the
railroad track, landing a couple hundred feet from the house. No one else in that area had that much
damage.

There was also some damage from the strong southerly winds in the Edwards School area on
the southern side of West Main Street between South Taft Street and South Horn Street. Similar to
the Joiner School, there was a primary brick school building and two frame buildings that were used
as schools nearby. One of the frame buildings was northeast of the brick building and next to the
West Main Street-South Horn Street intersection. The building had a front door and a porch on the
western side, a hall across the building, and two classrooms, one on the northern side and one on the
southern side.

Zella Boner, a third-grade student in the south classroom, noticed it was fairly sunny around
noon, but later in the afternoon, it began to get very dark as the tornado was approaching West
Frankfort. Zella and some other students were sitting by the windows on the southern side of the
classroom. The southerly winds got very strong. All of a sudden, hail began to fall and hit the south
windows, and the terrible sound of the wind and hail began to frighten some of the students.

The teacher, Miss Huffman, was on the northern side of the room and said, "You children by the
windows, come over here!"

Zella and others by the windows quickly came to Miss Huffman on the other side of the room.
The hail and wind began breaking out the south windows. When the wind was strongest, the porch
on the western side of the building was blown off. Finally, the hail and wind died down, and shortly
after that, the sun came back out. Fortunately, no one in the frame school was injured.

The West Frankfort High School was well away from where the tornado went across West
Frankfort. Blodwen Coleman, a student, was at the high school when the tornado occurred. She was

in class when her teacher and all the other teachers were called out to the hallway. When her teacher came back into the classroom, Blodwen and the other students were told to go to the assembly hall. As the students from Blodwen's class were going to the assembly hall, they saw a few coal miners.

They first thought there had been some type of disaster at the mine. As they went into the assembly hall and sat down with the other students, however, the principal, Mr. Wilson, told the students that there had been a terrible tornado on the western side of town and the coal miners who worked on the surface had come over to the school to let their children know that they were okay. The students were dismissed from school. Blodwen decided to hurry home because her family's house was on the western side of town on North Parkhill Street. When she got there, she found that her parents, Martha and John Coleman, were okay and their home had not been affected much. Just six bricks had been torn off their chimney. Blowden learned that the tornado had passed by within two or three blocks of their home.

About three blocks west of her family's home on North Taft Street was where her brother, Albert Coleman, and his wife lived. Albert's wife saw the tornado coming. She picked up her baby and took her into the living room. She was able to get behind a couch for protection. As the tornado came by, they were on its southern edge, and their home was damaged but not destroyed. The windows were blown into the house, and many pieces of the glass fell on to the couch. Fortunately, by being behind the couch, Albert's wife and very little baby were not hurt.

After the tornado, a large fire truck raced off from downtown to find where a fire was occurring. They first went southwest but then turned back north. They were driving north of North Horn Street when they noticed some smoke coming up somewhere north of United Mine Workers Hospital. As they approached West Lindell Street, they had to stop because many telephone poles had been blown on to North Horn Street. They went back south and crossed over to North Gardner Street to drive back north. When they got past West Fourth Street, they first saw a badly damaged home. Frank Bell's home on North Gardner Street had been blown off its foundation and badly damaged. Fortunately, none of the Bell family members were killed. Now the firefighters could see that the smoke was coming out of one of the houses farther north that the tornado had destroyed.

In the new addition area, there was so much damage and so many people injured or killed that some family members did not know where other family members were located for a long time. For several babies who had been injured and were being held in a hospital or another city building, the people taking care of them in those buildings were not able to find who their parents and family members were for several days. In most of these cases, the babies parents either had been badly injured and taken somewhere else or they had been killed. Also, some of the Orient Mine #2 workers who were in good shape because they had been in the mine were not able to find some of their family members who had been at their homes when they were destroyed. Two of these mine workers were Clyde Reed and Fred Taylor.

Clyde Reed's home on North Illinois Street was demolished. His wife saw the tornado coming, placed her seven-week-old daughter, Peggy, onto a pillow, and started taking her across a hallway to a safer place. However, the tornado started destroying the house before she got there. She became unconscious as debris fell on her, and she was severely injured. When she recovered her consciousness, she found that the baby had disappeared. She learned her daughter, Fay, and her son, Arthur, had also been injured. Her husband was working in Orient Mine #2 when the tornado came through, and he was not hurt. He came home and found that his home had been destroyed and his family injured. His wife was in critical condition, and she had not been able to search very much for the baby. When Clyde found this out, he started looking through the debris nearby but could not find her. During the next few days, he checked with anyone in the vicinity who was caring for an infant to see if it might be his baby. He checked the hospitals and other buildings where children were being held and visited the morgues to see if he could find his baby daughter there. He also went out of town to a couple places where he heard the tornado had blown young children. However, even three days after the tornado occurred, he could still not find his baby daughter. Late on Saturday afternoon, relief workers were removing debris from the Clyde's place, and they found the Reed's young baby, who was dead.

The tornado also destroyed Fred and Stena Taylor's home on North Horn Street. Stena was severely injured and died later. When Fred got home, he could not find their five-year-old daughter, Geraldine. Two days after the storm, Fred went to Benton, trying to find his daughter. However, he was not able to find her. Later, he learned that Geraldine had been killed.

Many other family homes in the new addition area were completely destroyed. Some of them were the Clarks, the Woods, the Littles, the Scotts, the Grzanichs, the Mazes, and the Stokes. On West Eighth Street, Elisha and Emma Clark's had a home/grocery store. On the day of the tornado, their daughter, Lelia, and her husband, Walter Smith, were there with their three children. As the tornado was about to hit the Clark's home, Elisha and all of his family members were in the kitchen. The window in the front of the house was blown inside, and Elisha was blown behind the counter in the grocery room. He hung on to that area as hard as he could, but he was blown away as the house was destroyed. He looked around after he landed and found he was on top of a pile of uprooted apple trees that had been blown into his yard. He was injured and later found out that his daughter and his wife had been killed and the rest of his family members injured.

Mr. and Mrs. Tom Woods and Mr. and Mrs. Tom Little occupied a double house on North Parkhill Street. It was demolished, and all four people were severely injured when they were pinned under the ruins of the house. The debris immediately caught fire, and the people shouted for help. An Italian man nearby heard them shouting, and he crawled over the ruins. He was able to tear off some of the wreckage and help them get out.

The home of Charles and Della (Mick) Scott on North Douglas Street was also demolished. Della was killed. Charles and his five-year-old son, Charles Coy, were seriously injured. Charles and Della's daughter, Valena May, was at Edwards School when the tornado destroyed their home, so she was not injured.

Jack and Carolina Grzanich's home on North Parkhill Street was destroyed. All the family members were in their home when the tornado destroyed it. They all had some injuries, but fortunately, no one was severely injured or killed.

The home of Walter Aydelott on West Sixth Street was destroyed. His older relative, Sarah Aydelott, was killed. The homes of Claude Maze and O.A. Stokes on West Tenth Street were both destroyed. Claude Maze, his wife, and their two-year-old son, Billy, were in their house when the tornado hit it. Mrs. Maze was injured when she was caught underneath the falling debris, but Claude and Billy were not injured.

Even though most of the homes and buildings in and near the new addition area were completely destroyed, a few were damaged but not completely blown down. Third Baptist Church, near the intersection of North Washington Boulevard and West Sixth Street, was blown off its foundation and damaged but still standing up. Also, Albert Hughes's home on North Hughes Street and George Mekota's home on West Ninth Street were badly damaged but not completely destroyed.

North of the new addition area and across the high-level train track, the Orient Mine #2 shafts and other buildings were located. The two shafts and the office building were badly damaged but not blown down. The water tower was blown down. Some train cars were blown off the high-level track, and one fell on several cars and badly damaged them. Most of the miners were in the mine when the tornado came through, so they were essentially in a "storm cellar" and did not get hurt.

Frankfort Township

From the northern part of West Frankfort to just west of Parrish

As the tornado roared across North Anna Street in West Frankfort, it entered Frankfort Township and continued causing widespread devastation. About ten more people were either instantly killed or badly injured and died later in this part of town.

Just after the tornado got over North Anna Street, it destroyed the Chicago and Eastern Illinois Railroad roundhouse, the yard office, and other railroad buildings. Once the debris fell down, some of it caught fire. Chloe Emmett Burns, a worker in the roundhouse, was killed when it was destroyed. Louis Carlton, who was in one of the railroad buildings, was also killed. About a half-mile north of the roundhouse, the tornado blew away three hundred feet of railroad track. Also in this area north of the roundhouse, at Middle Fork Big Muddy River, the railroad trestle was blown off its piers.

Well east of the railroad roundhouse and near the northern edge of West Frankfort, the Peabody Mine #19 buildings were near the southern edge of the tornado. Some of the buildings were damaged, but they did not receive as much damage as the Orient Mine #2 shafts and buildings, which were in the middle of the tornado path.

The Peabody Mine #19 building area damaged by the tornado.
(Photo courtesy of the Frankfort Area Genealogy Society)

After the tornado caused major destruction in West Frankfort, and had rushed over the swamp area along Ewing Creek, it began causing tremendous devastation to the Peabody Mine #18 shafts and buildings and the surrounding mining village known locally as Caldwell or Peabody #18. In this area, thirty-seven people were known to have either been instantly killed or badly injured and died later.

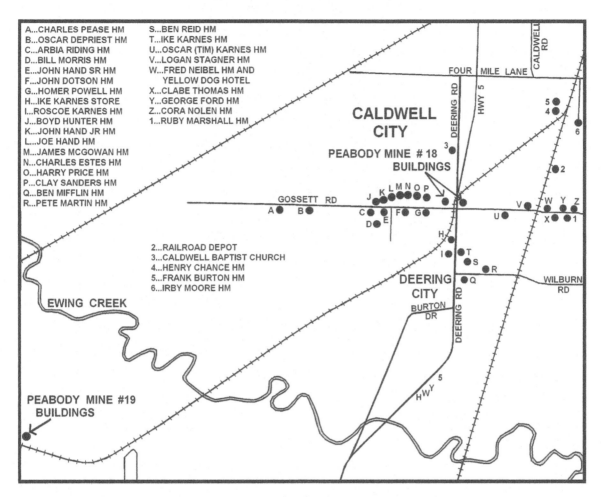

A...CHARLES PEASE HM
B...OSCAR DEPRIEST HM
C...ARBIA RIDING HM
D...BILL MORRIS HM
E...JOHN HAND SR HM
F...JOHN DOTSON HM
G...HOMER POWELL HM
H...IKE KARNES STORE
I...ROSCOE KARNES HM
J...BOYD HUNTER HM
K...JOHN HAND JR HM
L...JOE HAND HM
M...JAMES MCGOWAN HM
N...CHARLES ESTES HM
O...HARRY PRICE HM
P...CLAY SANDERS HM
Q...BEN MIFFLIN HM
R...PETE MARTIN HM

S...BEN REID HM
T...IKE KARNES HM
U...OSCAR (TIM) KARNES HM
V...LOGAN STAGNER HM
W...FRED NEIBEL HM AND
     YELLOW DOG HOTEL
X...CLABE THOMAS HM
Y...GEORGE FORD HM
Z...CORA NOLEN HM
1...RUBY MARSHALL HM

2...RAILROAD DEPOT
3...CALDWELL BAPTIST CHURCH
4...HENRY CHANCE HM
5...FRANK BURTON HM
6...IRBY MOORE HM

CALDWELL CITY

PEABODY MINE # 18 BUILDINGS

GOSSETT RD

FOUR MILE LANE

CALDWELL RD

DEERING RD

HWY 5

DEERING CITY

BURTON DR

WILBURN RD

EWING CREEK

PEABODY MINE #19 BUILDINGS

HWY 5

Black circle points that show tornado damage locations in the Peabody Mine # 18 area, and the mine villages know as Caldwell City and Deering City that are in western Frankfort Township.

The Peabody Mine #18 building area destroyed by the tornado.
(Photo courtesy of the Frankfort Area Genealogy Society)

James T. Carrier who was at home in August of 2007. He is showing his book called "Killer Tornado Hits Coal Mining Village" and he has much detailed information in his book about what happened in the Peabody Mine #18 village area. In his book he provides many interviews of local eyewitnesses who describe details about what happened when the tornado devastated the mine and the homes and buildings in the village area known as Caldwell and/or Deering City. (Photo courtesy of James T. Carrier, and taken by Bob Johns).

After the three-quarter to one-mile-wide tornado devastated the Peabody Mine #18 area, it continued across rural Frankfort Township. About a mile east of the Peabody Mine #18 area, on Warren Road south of Four Mile Lane, Walter and Edith Crawford lived in an old two-story house. On this day, Edith was there with her five-year-old daughter, Mary, and her two-year-old son, Clarence. Her eighteen-year-old brother, Frank Dillon, had come over to visit them. Edith noticed it had gotten very dark and cloudy in the afternoon, and she went outside several times to see the storm. The last time she went back inside, the tornado was approaching her home, and suddenly the front door in the living room was blown open. Frank picked up Mary, Edith picked up Clarence, and they tried to close the door. However, the wind was so strong they could not get it shut. The tornado hit, the living room started blowing apart, and that is the last thing they remembered before falling unconscious. When they were conscious again, they were lying on the floor and saw that the home's roof and walls were gone. Fortunately, they were only slightly injured. The heating stove had been blown to the corner of the floor, and it had set a rug on fire. However, it began raining hard, and the fire was stopped. Mary and Frank got up and noticed that, even though the barn was mostly blown away, part of it was tilted but not completely blown down. Edith and Frank picked up the children and ran over to get under the part of the barn that was still up to get out of the heavy rain.

Edith's husband had been working on the Peabody Mine #18 tipple when he saw the tornado approaching. He got down to the ground and ran over toward the washhouse. But he did not make it. Something hit his head, and he fell down. He saw an old coat blowing by, grabbed it, and put it over his head. Once the tornado was gone, he noticed that most buildings and homes in the area had been destroyed. Since his home was in the rural area about a mile east of where he was, he was worried that it might have been destroyed as well. He started running toward his home. As he was running over a field and got close to his home, he found it had been blown away. He started yelling for Edith. He finally found her and the other family members in the part of the barn that was still standing. He was really happy that they were not killed or badly injured.

He, Edith, and Frank looked around and found a table still standing on the floor with a pitcher of milk on it that had not been blown away. Mary noticed some chickens in the ditch by the home that did not have any feathers on them. Walter found that one of his horses had a board blown through its body. Later, he had to shoot it because it was in very bad shape and not likely to live very long.

Many days after the tornado had ended, one of their letters they had in their home had been sent back to them. It had been blown more than sixty miles away over into Indiana. Walter and Edith were very scared of storms for the rest of their lives. They built a storm cellar in their new home. Their daughter remembers that they went into the storm cellar every time it thundered, during day or night. Some of their neighbors came to get into their storm cellar as well.

*Walter and Edith Crawford and their children Mary and Clarence standing in their yard close to where their home was in the 1920s, and their home was completely destroyed by the tornado when it came by.
(Photo courtesy of "Mary Crawford" Cockrum)*

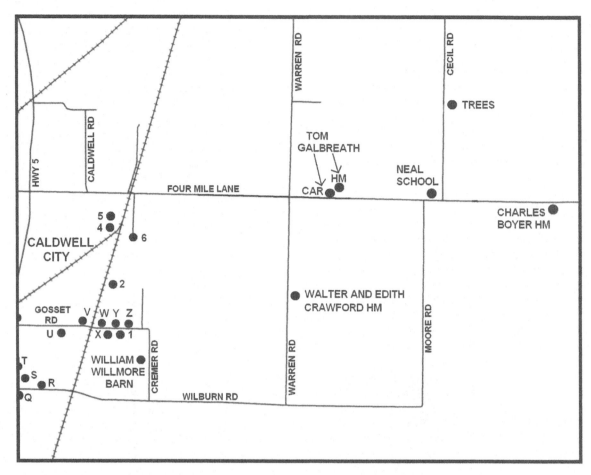

Black circle points that show tornado damage locations in central Frankfort Township which is just east of the Peabody Mine # 18 area and Caldwell City.

On Four Mile Lane, about a half-mile northeast of the Crawford's place, Neal School was located. On the day the tornado was approaching, the teacher sent the students home earlier than usual because it looked like it was somewhat stormy. He also left to go home in southern Hamilton County. When he got a few miles east of the school, he saw the tornado roaring by north of him. He was glad to see that it was not going toward his home and he hoped it had not hit any of his students' homes.

Two miles north of Neal School is where West Crown Point School was located in Benton Township. Easter Summers, a student, was in this school when the tornado came by. She and the other students were outside for their final recess. She saw the large, black tornado approaching from the west. Her teacher, Harley Neal, also saw it. He had Easter and all the other students come inside the school. Fortunately, the tornado passed by well south of their school.

Once the storm was gone, Harley let the students go home. Easter and her sister walked down to their parents' home, about a half-mile south of their school. Their father, Lawrence, was working at the Logan mine that day, but their mother, Emma, was at home when they got there. She mentioned to them that, when she saw the tornado approaching, she got out of their home and went across Cecil Road and got into a ditch. She was pleased that the tornado had not hit her home, but she knew it had passed by somewhere south of it. Easter wondered if the tornado had hit Neal School, about a mile and a half south of her home. Later, she and her sister were able to walk down Cecil Road to see if anything had happened to Neal School. As they got within a half-mile of Neal School, they started seeing some trees that had been blown down. When they got to the Neal School location, they saw it had been blown away with only the foundation left. They noticed one school seat still on the foundation. When Easter looked at the school's well, she noticed that all of the water had been sucked out of it. What Easter and her sister saw indicates that the Neal School teacher had made a good decision to have everyone leave the school long before the tornado destroyed it.

On the morning of March 18, 1925, Audie Wilburn and his brother-in-law, Harvey, drove up to north of Akin, where it was known that one of their relatives had died. While they were there during the afternoon, a storm came through, and they received very heavy rain and hail. They did not know that a tornado had passed south of them. When they started back home, they had to drive along or close to the tornado path from near Akin to where they lived in the West Frankfort area. They began noticing severe damage south of Akin, and when they got down to the northeastern part of Franklin Township, they had to stop because a destroyed home had been blown on to the road ahead of them. They returned to Parrish and tried to drive down another road. But again, after they drove for a while, another home was blown on to the road, and they could not go any farther. Audie decided to walk home. As he was walking down Four Mile Lane west of Logan Road, he noticed that Charles Boyer's barn and the roof of his home had been blown away. Audie heard somebody hollering, so he walked to the home to check on the Boyer family. He then realized that Charles and his wife could not get out of one of their rooms. Audie was able to go inside the house and found that a large post had been blown into the house and blocked the door to that room. He got the large wooden post off the door, and Charles and his wife were able to open the door and get out. Audie was pleased that he was able to help them.

Audie left the Boyer's farm and started walking back home on Four Mile Lane. After walking a half-mile, he saw that the Neal School had been blown away. As he continued walking along Four Mile Lane, he noticed that Tom and Betty Galbreath's home had been destroyed and Tom Galbreath's car had been blown southwest of his house. It had landed upside down in the ditch next to the road. When he finally got to the Peabody Mine #18 village area, he found that many homes had been destroyed. He was really worried that his family's home had been destroyed, too. However, when he got into West Frankfort, he found his home had not been damaged.

As the tornado moved on toward northeastern Frankfort Township and crossed Logan Road, it destroyed Dave and Eva Saxton's home on a hill of the Estese's farm and Lawrence Moore's home on his farm. Between the Moore's home and the Saxton's home, Parrish Road goes almost two miles east to Parrish, and the tornado destroyed everything on this road. On the first mile of Parrish Road between Logan Road and Kerley Road, at least ten people were killed. The first home destroyed along Parrish Road was Dan Joplin's home, which was on the southern side of the road, but fortunately, no one was killed there. The next home to the east was Joel and Margaret Crawford's home on their farm. When the tornado was approaching, Joel was not there. However, Margaret was, and her twenty-one-year-old daughter, Martha Braden, was visiting with her two children, Wilma and Roy, who were less than six years old. When the tornado hit their home, it was completely destroyed and blown away. Martha and her two children were killed instantly. Margaret was severely injured and died two days later.

East on along Parrish Road, on the Crawford's farm, was the home of their son, Johnny, and his wife, Essie. And a little farther east was Ted Kerley's home on his farm. Both of these homes were completely destroyed, but no one was killed. On Ted Kerley's farm, a two-by-four was blown completely through an oak tree. The next home along the road was James and Etta Kerley's home, which was on the northern side of the road. James was at work in the local mine area. However, Etta was home with her younger children. Two of her older sons, Otto and Homer, had gotten out of Oak Grove School and had either made it home or were still on their way when the tornado came through. James and Etta's home was completely destroyed, and Etta and her three-year-old daughter, Bertha, were killed when the home's porch fell onto them. Otto and Homer were badly injured and died shortly afterward. Her daughter, Pauline, was badly injured, with her head being cut from her jaw up to her ear.

Past the Kerley's home, on the southern side of Parrish Road, was William Rainey's home on the Darnell's farm. The tornado blew away the Rainey's home. William Rainey and his wife, Deboria, were also blown away. Deboria was killed when she landed on a clay bank not far from where their home had been. William was blown almost a quarter-mile to the southeast and was also killed when he landed on a tree next to where a creek crossed Kerley Road. His body was not found until several days later.

The Ted Kerley home destroyed by the tornado. (Photo courtesy of "Eula Kerley" Spain)

The James Kerley home destroyed by the tornado. (Photo courtesy of "Eula Kerley" Spain)

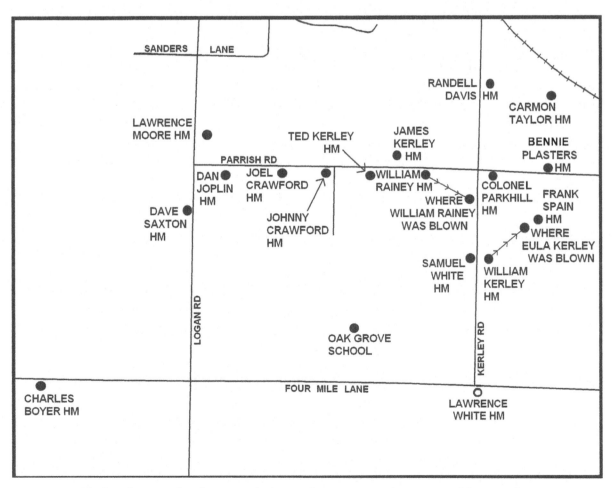

Black circle points that show tornado damage locations in northeastern Frankfort Township.
Two of black circle points show where people landed after they were blown away from their homes.
The white circle point shows where a home was not hit by the tornado and not damaged.

While the tornado had destroyed every building along the first mile of Parrish Road, it also damaged and demolished several homes, barns, and other buildings on Kerley Road north and south of Parrish Road. More than a quarter-mile to the north on Kerley Road was Randall Davis's home. It was badly damaged when the tornado came through. More than a quarter-mile to the south on Kerley Road were William "Bill" and Nellie Kerley's home and outbuildings on the eastern side and Samuel and Elizabeth White's home and outbuildings on the western side. Samuel and Elizabeth White were Nellie Kerley's parents.

During the day when the tornado occurred, Bill and Nellie's son, Jewell, and daughters, Reathel and Eula, were at Oak Grove School, about a half-mile to the southwest of their home. Eight-year-old Eula and her cousin, Glorine Summers, were able to leave the school early because they did not need to be in the last class when geography was being taught to the older students. They thought about staying near the school and playing in the big ditch until the school finally closed and the other students came by, but they decided to go on home promptly because it was getting cloudy and looked like it was going to rain. Glorine lived with her grandparents, Samuel and Elizabeth White, so she and Eula walked together to their homes on Kerley Road. They first stopped at Glorine's home, but then they both walked across the street to Eula's home because Eula's mother was making a dress for Glorine.

Just after Eula and Glorine got there, it was starting to get very dark and a little stormy outside. Eula's uncle and aunt, Frank "Fritz" and Drusilla "Drew" Spain, were very scared of storms, and they decided to leave their home and go over to Bill and Nellie's home to seek shelter in their storm cellar. When they got there and it was getting stormier, Nellie decided to take everyone down to the storm cellar. However, the tornado was coming so fast that they did not get to the storm cellar before it hit their home. Eula was in the front bedroom when the tornado was about to hit. She was looking out the window and saw some debris flying up high in the air, but she could not see the tornado because nearby tall trees were blocking her view to the west. All of a sudden, she saw the window blow out and her mother's big fern next to the window blow over. She quickly ran toward the room where her mother and the others were getting ready to go to the storm cellar. However, before she got there, she saw the dining room table and its cloth get blown through a double window. That is the last thing she remembered as she, the others, and the home were being completely blown away.

After the tornado had destroyed Bill and Nellie's home and rushed away to the east-northeast, Eula recovered her consciousness and found she was on the ground between a creek and the area where Fritz and Drew lived, about a quarter-mile northeast. Eula noticed something had hit her, she had lost her two front teeth, and her chin below her mouth had been cut open. She was able to feel that her tongue would easily stick through the cut chin, which really scared her. She got up and saw that Fritz and Drew's home had been very badly damaged and that Glorine had been dropped nearby. Glorine did not think she could get up, but she was able to do so shortly after Eula came. Eula and Glorine started running back toward Eula's home.

Halfway there, they found Eula's aunt lying on her back with a two-by-four that had been blown into her head. Her head had been split open, and she was in very bad shape. Even though Drew had been blown a long way from Eula's home, Eula was able to find a rug nearby that had been blown from her home, and she tried to cover Drew with it. But since Eula was only eight years old, there was nothing else she knew she could do to help her. Also, Eula was worried that her mother might have been killed. So she and Glorine began running again toward Eula's home. Once they got to where the home was supposed to be, they only saw the home's foundation. The top of the storm cellar had been torn off, and a can of fruit that had been placed inside of it had been damaged. No one was in the storm cellar, so they started looking around and could not find Nellie anywhere near. They looked farther away and finally found her well south of the house. She was still on the ground where she had landed, and she was holding her little baby, Eldon, who was playing with a stick and hitting some water right next to them.

Hen egg-sized hailstones had hit Nellie after she landed on the ground. Eula and Glorine saw that some of the hailstones were still on her. One was on her head near her hairline. Eula helped get that hailstone off of her. The hailstones had badly bruised Nellie's arms and some other parts of her body.

Eula was glad to find that her mother and baby brother had not been killed. Nellie was able to get up, and all of them went to where Nellie's home had been to see if they could find the others. They did see Nellie's parents, Samuel and Elizabeth, walking toward them. Samuel and Elizabeth were holding each other up because they had been injured when the tornado blew away their home. Similarly to Nellie's home, only the foundation was still there.

Eula's older brother, Jewell, had gotten back from Oak Grove School, where he had stayed for the last class. He told Eula, "After you were gone, the tornado hit the school and I was blown out in the yard when it was destroyed. It was really good that Arlie Moore grabbed me and took me farther away after I landed. I had landed under the huge oak tree and it was blown down just after I was away from there. I might have been killed if I was still where I landed."

Shortly later, Eula felt it was so beautiful to see the sun had come out. That really meant the storm was over. When her father, Bill, got back from the mine near Logan, he and Nellie decided they would take Eula and the rest of their family down to the home of Nellie's brother, Lawrence White, which the tornado had not damaged. However, their daughter, Reathel, had not made it back from Oak Grove School yet. They learned from someone that Reathel and some other students had been taken to a nearby undamaged home after the school was destroyed. When they went to this home to pick up Reathel, they found she had been injured when large bricks from chimney of the school's heating stove fell on her as the tornado destroyed the school. After Bill and Nellie picked up Reathel, they took their entire family to Lawrence's home, about a half-mile south of where their home had been. When they got there, Lawrence's wife, Grace, said they could stay as long as they needed to, but she was worried about her husband since he was over at Peabody Mine #18 and had not got home yet. When Lawrence did get home, they found he had been injured when the tornado destroyed the mine area. His face was cut open. However, he was pleased that his home was in good shape and his wife and family members had not been very badly injured or killed.

Eula's family stayed at Lawrence and Grace's home for several days. Then her family had a tent built near where their home had been and stayed there until they got a new home built. Eula and her family were very afraid of storms after this event, and they went into their storm cellar every time they thought a bad storm was coming.

"Eula Kerley" Spain shown inside her home in April of 2007. She was in her family's home when the tornado destroyed it back in 1925, and she was blown about a quarter of a mile away from where the home was destroyed by the tornado. (Photo courtesy of "Eula Kerly" Spain, and taken by Bob Johns)

After the tornado had destroyed and blown away many homes and killed and injured people along the first mile of Parrish Road and parts of Kerley Road, it continued to be very devastating along and near Parrish Road as it raced toward the town of Parrish. The first home along Parrish Road after crossing Kerley Road was Colonel and Ella Parkhill's home, which was on their farm. Colonel, Ella, and their daughter-in-law, Madge, were standing on their back porch watching the big storm as it arrived. Their home was blown away, and they were blown into their yard. Ella was badly injured, but Colonel and Madge were only slightly injured. Most of Madge's clothes had been blown off of her. She decided to walk to the mine area near Logan to let her husband, Clyde Parkhill, and other miners know what had happened on Parrish Road. As she was walking there, she found a neighbor's undamaged home, where she found some clothes to put on.

On Parrish Road, about a quarter-mile east of the destroyed Parkhill's home, was Bennie Plaster's home, which was also destroyed. North of Bennie's home was Carmon Taylor's home, which was destroyed as well. Carmon's wife was badly injured, and her two young sons, Merl and Kenneth, were killed.

As the tornado reached Baseline Road on the eastern edge of Frankfort Township, it destroyed John Ross's home on the southwestern side of the intersection with Parrish Road. Somewhere north of Parrish Road, more likely in Frankfort Township than Cave Township, it was found that Charles, Christina, and Eva Gunter were killed when the tornado destroyed a home they were in.

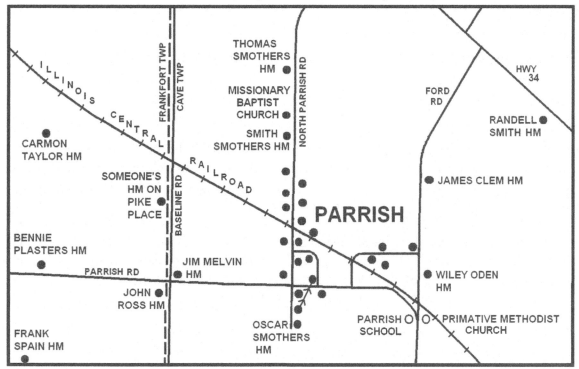

Black circle points that show tornado damage locations in the northeast edge of Frankfort Township and northwestern Cave Township including the town of Parrish. Two white circle points show where things were not hit by the tornado and were not damaged. More details about Parrish are on the next map.

As the tornado roared across Frankfort Township and devastated many places, sixty-two people were either instantly killed or badly injured and died later. About ten of these people were in the northern part of West Frankfort. Thirty-seven were in the Peabody Mine #18 village area; fifteen were in the area along and north of Parrish Road.

Cave Township

From just west of Parrish to east-northeast of Parrish

As the tornado entered Cave Township, it destroyed Jim and Ida Melvin's home, which was on the northeastern side of the intersection of Parrish Road and Baseline Road. Their thirteen-year-old daughter, Lola, was blown away from the home as it was being destroyed. As she was blown away from the home, she noticed a cow near her that was also getting blown through the air. Fortunately, when Lola fell onto the ground, she was not injured very much.

After continuing along Parrish Road, the three-quarter- to one-mile-wide tornado entered the town of Parrish and began destroying many of the homes and buildings. Joe Melvin's home in the southwestern part of town was destroyed, and both Joe and his wife, Eva, were killed. Larkin Cantrell's home in the northwestern part of town was blown away, and Larkin's mother, Belle McFarland, who lived there, was killed. Also, Larkin's wife, Matt, was badly injured when a silver plate was blown into her head.

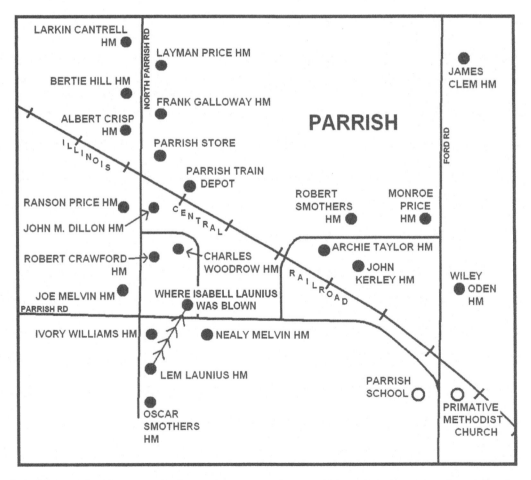

Black circle points that show tornado damage locations in the town of Parrish in Cave Township. A line from one black circle point to another black circle point shows where a lady got blown away from, and where she landed. Two white circle points show where things were not hit by the tornado and were not damaged.

In the center of town, the train depot next to the railroad was blown away, and station agent, Ivory Williams, was blown out to near the train track. Ivory's wife was looking for him and found him lying below wires from a telegraph pole. She saw he was crushed and burned. He died a few hours later after he had been taken to Benton.

Near the train depot, Clarence Lowman and his father-in-law, James Clem, were running the general store. Clarence saw the whirling black funnel approaching and warned James. He then started running toward his home, which was on the northwestern side of town, but the tornado immediately overtook him. He laid down next to the railway and held on to the rail to keep from being blown away. Although he was able to keep holding on to the rail, the strong wind blew things on him, and he was badly injured. He was later taken to a hospital in Benton and found out that his home in the northwestern part of town was one of the few that were not badly damaged and his family members were not injured. James Clem was also badly injured when the general store was destroyed. Unlike Clarence, he found that his home, which was on the northeastern edge of town, was completely destroyed and his wife, Gertie, was killed.

Looking east to where the Parrish Train Depot was destroyed by the tornado.
(Photo courtesy of the Frankfort Area Genealogy Society)

Parrish Store completely destroyed by the tornado. (Photo courtesy of the Frankfort Area Genealogy Society)

North of the general store, Frank and Lou Ella Galloway's home was destroyed, and just north of their home, the home of their daughter, Beaulah, and her husband, Layman Price, was destroyed. Lou Ella, and her son, Royal Eugene, Layman, Beaulah, and their son, Jackie, were all killed instantly. Badly injured Frank was taken to Benton, where he died several days later. Most of these people were in their homes when the tornado hit, but those who were not home were somewhere else in Parrish.

Smith Smother's home, north of Larkin Cantrell's home, was also destroyed. Smith's wife, Opal, had her daughter, Helen Brown, and Helen's one-year-old-baby over for a visit from Logan. While Helen was in the yard and had just finished some washing, she noticed that it was getting dark and starting to thunder. The lightning became so frequent that she got scared and went into the house. She went into the bedroom to check on her baby, who was asleep. When she got near his bed, a tree from the front yard suddenly crashed through the front of the living room where Opal was. She grabbed her baby and jumped behind the bedroom door. The door, however, fell down on top of them, and the whole house was destroyed. Fortunately, she and her son and mother were not hurt much.

On the southwestern edge of town was Lem Launius's home. On the day the tornado was coming, Lem was working at the mine area in Logan, and several of his children, including nine-year-old Gustavia, were at Parrish School. At his home were his wife, Isabelle, his five-year-old son, Wayne, and his daughter, Alta, who was living there with her baby. As the tornado was approaching, Isabelle ran outside and grabbed Wayne. She brought him back inside and held the door shut as the tornado was about to hit their home. Wayne held on to her dress. Alta was holding her baby in the front bedroom, and she yelled for her mother to come to her. The home started blowing apart, and the tornado was demolishing it. Isabelle was blown away, but Wayne was left there in the debris. As the home was being blown away, Alta lost her consciousness, and when she woke up, she was lying on the ground fairly close to the home's foundation, and still holding her baby. She was not sure what had happened, and she and her baby did not seem to be hurt. Since it was hailing on her and a rug had been blown onto her, she stayed under the rug with her baby until the hail finally quit. Then she got up from under the rug and saw that their home had been blown away. There was nothing left but some pieces of lumber. She saw Wayne lying on some lumber where the house had been. She noticed that one of his ears had been almost cut off, but he did not seem to have any other problems. She wondered where her mother was but could not find her on the home's foundation or in their yard.

Two other homes were on the short street where her family's home had been. She looked north and saw that Ivory Williams's home had been blown away. Then she looked south and saw that Oscar Smothers's home had been twisted all the way around on the foundation and badly damaged, but it was not completely destroyed. She was not able to find her mother, and she was really worried about her.

Lem finished his mine work in Logan, and he was unaware that a tornado had devastated Parrish. As usual, he got off work and began walking southeast along the railroad track toward Parrish, about two miles from Logan. As he got closer to Parrish, he started to see pieces of debris lying on the ground near the railroad track. After he walked a little farther, he started seeing that the nearby trees had been blown down. When he saw Parrish, he was amazed that most of the homes and buildings appeared to have been demolished. He was worried about his family members and moved faster to get into town. When he got there and was walking as fast as he could toward his home on the southern side of town, he saw that his friend, Poppy, had his home destroyed. Poppy was in his yard, and when he saw Lem, he rushed over to meet with him. Poppy told him that his wife, Isabelle, had been killed and her body was lying on the edge of the street near his home. He took Lem over to where his wife was. Lem saw that her body had been badly cut up. She had been blown more than three hundred feet northeast of where their home was located. He picked her up and took her with him to his home to find out about the rest of the family. Fortunately, even though he found that his home had been blown away, he soon found out that the rest of his family members were alive and not badly injured.

Most of the buildings in Parrish were completely flattened or blown away. Only a few were damaged but still standing. Only two buildings within the town appeared to be not damaged at all: Primitive Methodist Church and Parrish School. Both were on the southeastern edge of town.

The school was a big building, but it was a one-room school. On the day of the tornado, about thirty-five to forty students were in school. Two of the students were Gustavia Launius, Lem and Isabelle's nine-year-old daughter, and Lovell Woodrow, Charles and Stella Woodrow's eleven-year-old daughter. Their teacher was Delmer Perryman. Lovell and her brother, Nealy Ray, went home for lunch near midday and then returned to the school. Lovell noticed it was beginning to get dark outside. After they got back to school and Delmer was teaching some of his students in the afternoon, everyone in the school noticed it was getting almost as dark as night outside. It was also getting very dark inside because, in 1925, the school did not have electricity. Delmer realized a bad storm was coming because it was so dark. He could also hear what sounded like a train out to the west, but there was no real train, not even on the railroad track just east of them. He was very worried about what might happen to them. He asked all of the students to get away from the windows on the western side of the room and come over to where he was, in a corner of the room. When Gustavia got to him, she noticed that Delmer was very worried, but she was not scared because she did not know what was happening. However, Lovell was scared because she could hear the train sound getting very loud. She realized it was a very bad storm. She held her brother in her arms as she stood by the teacher. Fortunately, the school windows did not get blown out, and the school seemed okay. However, even though the train sound was starting to be less loud, it began hailing and pouring down rain.

While it was still hailing and raining, someone was banging on the door. The teacher let the man in, and Lovell noticed it was her father. Charles said to the teacher "Almost everything in town has been blown away and you should keep the children in the school until it is safer for them to go outside." The teacher kept the students in the school until it looked safe to let them out.

"Gussie Launius" Hieple shown in her home in May of 2007. She was in the Parrish Church when the tornado came close by in 1925. (Photo courtesy of "Gussie Launius" Hieple, and taken by Bob Johns)

"Lovell Woodrow" Carlile shown in her home in May of 2007. She was in the Parrish Church when the tornado came close by in 1925. (Photo courtesy of "Lovell Woodrow" Carlile, and taken by Bob Johns)

When they were able to leave, Gustavia and her two sisters left to walk through the field that was between the school and their home on the southwestern edge of the town. Once they got to where their home had been and saw it had been blown away, they were really worried about their mother and others who had been there. They later found out that their mother had been killed and their young brother had been injured.

Lovell's uncle came over to the school to take Lovell and Nealy Ray back home. As they left the school, Lovell saw many completely destroyed homes and debris as they walked across the town. When she got near her family's home, she saw someone else's home had been blown right next to her family's home. It was badly damaged but still had some of its rooms and part of its roof connected. She would later learn that it was Ivory Williams's home. It had been blown several hundred feet from the southwest. Lovell saw that her family's home had been damaged, but she was pleased that it had not been blown away and was still standing. She also noticed that Robert Crawford's home was still standing and only slightly damaged.

When she found her family members who had been home, she learned that none had been injured. Her mother, Stella, told her that, as the tornado was approaching, she and her son, Gene, who was sick, and several neighbors were in her home. They all got into the living room and held on to each other as the tornado was about to arrive. Stella was holding Gene as hard as she could. Then as the tornado hit her home, part of the roof was blown off, and several windows were blown out. The home's flue fell through the ceiling into the living room. It hit the arm of a couch, tore it off, and then fell on the floor. Fortunately, the flue or windows hurt no one in the living room.

Charles Woodrow's home in Parrish badly damaged, but not destroyed by the tornado.
(Photo courtesy of "Lovell Woodrow" Carlile)

Later in the day, an Illinois Central Railroad train came back to Parrish to pick up people and take them where they needed to go. The train had several flatcars and a caboose where they could place the people. Many of the injured were put in the caboose, and most of the dead were put on one of the flatcars. The rest were put on some of the flatcars. Gustavia Launius's dead mother, Isabelle, was put on a flatcar, and Gustavia and the rest of her family were on another. Lovell Woodrum and her family were put on a flatcar as well. It was now cold, and Lovell's family brought along some blankets and coats to wear while they were sitting on the open flatcar.

When the train stopped in Logan, Gustavia's family got off and met with her uncle, Raul Launius, who was there with his wagon to take them to his home. Lovell's family also got off at Logan and went to stay at her aunt's home.

After the debris was cleaned up in Parrish, tents were placed there for people to live in until they were able to get their homes fixed or new ones built. Lovell's father, Charles, went back to Parrish and placed a floor in their tent and some lumber around it. When Lovell was taken back to her family's tent in Parrish, she knew they would have to stay there until their damaged home was fixed. Sometimes she had trouble sleeping because the top of the tent would keep flopping and make noise when it was windy. When their home was fixed, Lovell was glad to be able to get back there. However, it would be a long time before she could shut out her thoughts of the terrible damage she had seen and her knowledge about the deaths, injuries, and other damage that had occurred in Parrish.

Other people who were known to have been killed by the tornado in Parrish were Andy Downs, Hannah Cunningham, Billie Cunningham, Raymond Price, a baby named Price, Mrs. Gray, and a black man. So it appears that this devastating tornado killed nineteen people in the small town of Parrish. Although it was mentioned in local newspapers that Ivan Smothers had been killed, it was later found that he had not ever been injured, as mentioned in the *Benton Evening News* on March 25, 1925.

As the tornado moved out of Parrish, one of the first farms hit was Randell Smith's place near Highway 34. Randell's home, barn, and other farm buildings were all destroyed. Randell and his wife, Bertha, were home with some of their children when the tornado hit. Their seven-year-old daughter, Hattie, was killed. All the others there were injured, and Randell lost his eyesight. Since he could not work on his damaged farm, the Boy Scouts from Benton and other places nearby came to help him and cleaned up a lot of the wreckage.

Randell Smith's home and buildings completely destroyed by the tornado.
(Photo courtesy of the Frankfort Area Genealogy Society)

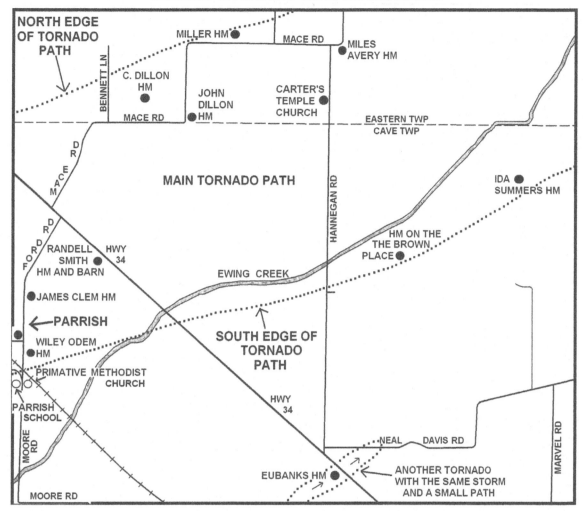

Black circle points that show tornado damage locations in northwest Cave Township east of Parrish and southwest Eastern Township. This map has path lines that show where the large tornado roared across this area and a small tornado occurred south of it.

More than a mile farther southeast of Randell Smith's farm along Highway 34 was the Eubanks's farm. The farm was far enough south that the tornado was passing by, and it seemed like the farm was safe. Parrish School, Primitive Methodist Church, and other places between this farm and the southern edge of the tornado path were safe because the tornado did not hit them. However, the Eubanks's home on his farm was completely destroyed at the same time as places farther north were. The storm that developed the large tornado also developed a small tornado that did not last long just south of Parrish while the large tornado was going through the town. Unfortunately, the Eubanks's home was located where this small tornado occurred.

After the long-lasting tornado had destroyed things on Randell Smith's farm and crossed Highway 34, it started to move into Eastern Township. However, it was still causing damage in Cave Township from just south to well north of Ewing Creek. A home near Ewing Creek and just east of Hannegan Road was destroyed. Farther northeast was Ida Summer's place. Ida was at home and sleeping upstairs when the tornado was coming. When it got there, it tore the roof off her house. Fortunately, she was not injured. She later noticed that her barn, which was south of her home, was not damaged. However, she also noticed a lot of damage north of her home. Her well, which was northwest of her home, had been badly damaged, and most of its bricks and some of its water had been blown away. She also saw that many trees had been damaged and broken down along and near Ewing Creek from east to north of her place and debris in the trees that were still standing. The debris in the trees could still be seen for many years.

To the northeast of Ida's place, near Green Meadow Road and right next to the Cave-Eastern Township line, was Alex Summer's home. After the tornado had torn the roof off Ida's home, it completely destroyed Alex's home. Fortunately, no one was killed. This was the last place that the tornado destroyed in Cave Township. By that time, twenty people in Cave Township had either been instantly killed or had been badly injured and died later.

Eastern Township

From east-northeast of Parrish to the county line east southeast of Akin

As the three-quarter- to one-mile-wide tornado reached Eastern Township, one of the first places hit was John Dillon's farm, next to where Mace Road turned north off the Cave-Eastern Township line. John's home was completely blown away, and his barn and other outbuildings on his farm were destroyed. Fortunately, no one was killed. C. Dillion's home northwest of John's farm was damaged but not destroyed. North of John's farm, on the northern side of Mace Road, the northern edge of the tornado damaged the Miller's home only slightly. It was bent over a little to the south, but there was no other damage.

Along Hannegan Road, Carter's Temple Church was destroyed. On the church's small graveyard, one gravestone was blown over. Fortunately, no one was in the church, and no one was injured or killed. Farther north, near where Hannegan Road meets Mace Road, is where Miles Avery's home was located. The tornado completely destroyed his home, and Miles, his wife, Nancy, and their daughter were severely injured.

As the tornado raced across Eastern Township, many more people were in danger. When it approached Green Meadow Road and the Mount Etna community, it first hit Gilbert Shew's farm and blew away his home. Gilbert was very severely injured and later had to be taken to his father's home south of Benton. He died about three years later. As the tornado reached the western side of Green Meadow Road, the farms of Gilbert's brothers, Clyde and Arthur, were both badly affected. From their home, Clyde and his wife, Vera, saw it was very dark west of them and it was getting stormy. They decided to get their children, who were not at school, together with them in the house. Just after that, they started hearing a loud noise coming from the storm. They looked out a window and saw a tornado coming toward them, and it was throwing debris in the air from the Carter's Temple Church area. This really worried them, so they quickly took their children with them into the storm cellar. After that, the tornado hit their home and completely blew it away. Fortunately, they were not injured.

Farther north at Arthur Shew's farm, Arthur's wife, Clella, was the only family member there as the tornado was approaching. When it hit their farm, the home, the barn, and all of the outbuildings were blown away. Clella was blown out of the house, and one of the walls fell onto her. When some people came to find the Shews, they found that the only thing still standing was a toilet. As they were looking around the area, they found Clella lying under the wall. She was very badly injured, so they tried to take her to a neighbor's house. However, Clella passed away before they could get there.

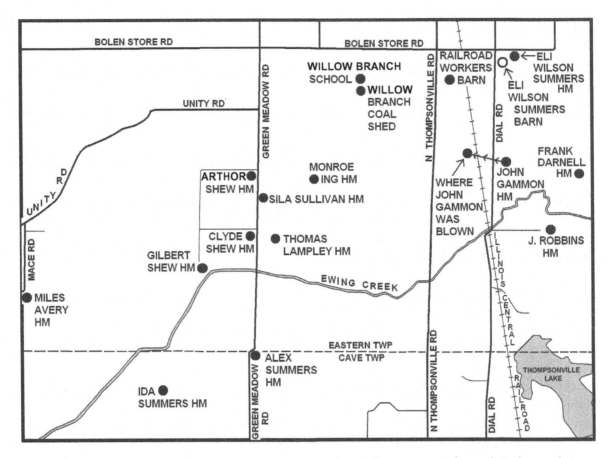

Black circle points that show tornado damage locations in south central Eastern Township and north central Cave Township. A line from one black circle point to another black circle point shows where a man got blown away from, and where he landed. One white circle point shows where a barn was not damaged by the tornado.

On the eastern side of Green Meadow Road, the tornado hit several more homes. Thomas Lampley's home was completely wrecked, and he was seriously injured. Sila Sullivan's home was destroyed, and his wife, Rhoda, was seriously injured and taken to the nearby home of Charles Downes. Monroe Ing's home was also destroyed, and his wife, Mary, was killed.

North of Monroe's home and closer to Bolen Store Road was Willow Branch School. On the day of the tornado, the teacher, Mr. Wormley, and his two children rode to school on a buggy with a team of horses. When they got there, he put the horses in a coal shed that was just south of the school and left his buggy next to the shed. Then he went in to teach the students, including his children. During the afternoon, it began to get dark. A couple of the older girls were looking out a window on the southern side of the building and saw the tornado coming. It really scared them, and they started crying. Mr. Wormley had all the students lie down in a corner of the building. Then he got down on his knees and started praying. As the tornado went by, the school was shaking, and everyone was scared. Afterward, it stayed noisy because it started hailing, and the hail was hitting the roof and the walls. Finally, the hail quit, and it started getting sunny outside. Mr. Wormley took the students back to where he could continue his teaching work. But then one of the neighbors, covered in mud, opened the school door, stuck his head in, and said that any of the students who lived west of the school should know that their homes had been destroyed and they should go home now. All of the students left to go home because they were worried about what had happened to their families.

Mr. Wormley decided he would take his children home. As he went outside, he noticed that the school had been pushed a couple of inches to the south on its foundation. It was slightly damaged. As he was going to get his horses and the buggy, he saw that the coal shed, the horses, and the buggy had all been blown away. This really worried him. He and his children started searching for the horses and the buggy. They finally did find them, and even though the horses were injured and the buggy slightly damaged, they were able to set up things to go home. Mr. Wormley was really glad that Willow Branch School was far enough north of the tornado path that it was not damaged much.

Railroad workers were building a railroad near Thompsonville Road across Eastern Township. They had rented an old house and a barn to place things in that they were using to build the railroad. On the day of the tornado, some had gone south of Thompsonville with their bulldozer to get some coal. When the tornado was approaching, they were driving their bulldozer up Dial Road with the coal. However, when they got just north of Ewing Creek, they saw it was going to hit them. They stopped their bulldozer on the road and hung on to it. Although they were slightly injured with debris, the heavy bulldozer did not get turned over, and they did not blow away. After the tornado had gone away, they went to their rented house to see if the tornado had hit the other workers. They saw that the barn had been destroyed, but fortunately, the house was not damaged, and the workers there had not been injured.

The tornado hit several houses near Dial Road and Ewing Creek. The home of J. Robbins, which was east of Dial Road and south of Ewing Creek, was destroyed, and Frank Darnell's home, which was east of Dial Road and north of Ewing Creek, was destroyed. On Dial Road and just north of Ewing Creek, John Gammon's house had been torn to pieces, and all the lumber from the house had been blown to the western side of the road.

John had rented this house from Florence Summers. After the tornado, Florence came to see what had happened. She found John's wife and his daughter, Susan, near the house. One had a broken arm; the other had her hair tangled up. She could not find John anywhere. However, she was glad to find that the home of her brother, Eli Wilson Summers, and his family was not destroyed. Their home was farther north on Dial Road, next to the intersection with Bolen Store Road. Florence took John's wife and her daughter to Eli's home, where they would have a place to stay.

Sometime during the late afternoon, one of the railroad workers found John on the ground near the railroad. He was very badly injured. He had been blown almost a quarter-mile west of his home. The workers decided to pick him up and take him to Eli Wilson Summers's home, where John's wife and daughter had already been taken.

As the tornado was approaching, Eli Wilson Summers saw the storm coming toward his farm. His wife, Nellie, and his oldest daughter, Agnus, had gone to Akin. Two of his sons, Dempsey and Paul, were at Willow Branch School. His oldest son, Oren, and some of his little children were there with him as the tornado was coming. Eli and Oren took the little children to the bottom part of his old log barn because it was the safest place to be. After they got into the barn, a neighbor lady arrived at their place. She was scared as she saw this storm coming. Just as she got to Eli's yard but not yet to his house, the tornado had arrived. She saw a big tree in the backyard get blown off the ground and across the house. It hit the roof and took off part of it. As she got to the house, she saw that all of the doors had been blown open, but no family members were there. She was scared, but when the tree was blown away, the tornado was mostly going by to the south of Eli's yard. That was why the barn was not damaged, the house was only slightly damaged, and she was not injured.

The barn shown in April of 2007. This barn is where Eli Summers took his children for safety when the 1925 tornado was coming towards them. (Photo Courtesy of Dempsey Summers, and taken by Bob Johns)

After the tornado had gone, Eli and the others in the old log barn went back into the house, and the neighbor lady decided to go home to check on her place. Dempsey and Paul Summers were let out of school and ran home. Nellie and Agnus made it back from Akin. Eli was pleased to find that none of his family members were hurt. However, they did have a problem in their home. The tree had torn off part of the roof, and a lot of rain and hail had fallen into the house. After the rain and hail had ended, Oren spent some time drilling holes into the floor to let out the water. Finally, the floor dried. When the home was in a better shape, the family was taking care of the Gammons who had been brought to their home. The Summers family was able to set up some beds for the Gammons that night. John Gammon was not feeling well. He had a cut on his back, just under his shoulder blade. He also had some blood coming out of his mouth, and he had a lung problem. After he had been placed in a bed, Dempsey put some pillows on him so he could feel better. Although this was helpful, he was so badly injured that he died sometime during the night.

Dempsey Summers shown in his home in April of 2007. He was in the Willow Branch School when it was slightly damaged by the tornado in 1925. (Photo Courtesy of Dempsey Summers, and taken by Bob Johns)

Farther east in Eastern Township, the tornado destroyed a lot more homes and buildings. Along Hoover Road, the tornado destroyed William Tanner's home and the nearby Puckett home, but fortunately, no one was killed. Farther north on Hoover Road, Knob Prairie School, known as Buckoo School, was located. On this day, the teacher at the school, George Huffstuttier, noticed a bad storm was coming. He sent the younger students home. As the storm got closer and he recognized it was a tornado, he decided to take the older students out and into one of the lower outside toilets, which were safer to be in. He was able to get most of the students into the boys' outside toilet, which was southwest of the school. Just after they got there, the tornado roared through the area and destroyed the girls' outside toilet and the school. Fortunately, the boys' toilet was not blown away. George and the students he had there were not badly hurt. However, the students, Delila Galbraith and Robert Akins, had not made it out of the school when the tornado arrived. As the school was blown away, they were blown across the road and landed in a wooded area.

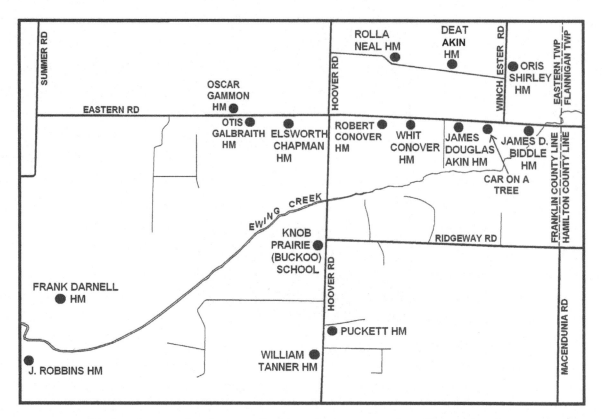

Black circle points that show tornado damage locations in southeast Eastern Township.

Mae Galbraith, Delila's sister, was one of the younger students that George Huffstudttier had sent home when he first saw the storm coming. After she had walked north on Hoover Road for a few hundred yards, her father, Otis Galbraith, who was working on an old house nearby, found her. He started taking Mae on farther north toward their home. But he shortly decided they were going the wrong way and, to stay away from the tornado, they should go back south. Just before they got to the school, Otis realized the tornado was going to hit them. He put Mae down next to a fence and put a coat on her. Then he held on to her and the fence. Everything around there was torn up, but the fence was not damaged, and they were not hurt. After the storm, Otis decided he and Mae should go to Eastern Road to see if their home and other family members were okay. When they got up to the Hoover Road-Eastern Road intersection and went west on Eastern Road, they saw that Elsworth Chapman's home was badly damaged and the barn destroyed. They saw that Oscar Gammon's home, just northwest of their home, had been destroyed. Fortunately, they saw that their home was not damaged very much at all. When they got into their home, they found that none of their family members there had been injured. However, Otis did find that his daughter, Delila, had not gotten home from the school. He decided to go back to the school to find her. When he got back, he found people near where the school had been, and George had told him to find where Delila and Robert were. So Otis started looking for them, too. After a while, they found them in a wooded area on the eastern side of Hoover Road. Delila and Robert were still unconscious, and they had been badly injured. Otis and one of the others took Delila and Robert to a hospital. Fortunately, both were able to get better within a few days.

After the tornado crossed Hoover Road, a lot of destruction was along and north of Eastern Road. Robert and Mary Conover's home was the first one hit, and it was completely destroyed. To the east of Robert Conover's home lived his uncle and aunt, Whit and Evaline Conover. They were in their home when the tornado completely destroyed it. They were blown into their yard and very badly injured. Whit died from his injuries a few days later.

To the east of the Conover's home lived James Douglas "Doug" and Emma Akin. On the day of the tornado, Doug and Emma left their home and walked northwest for a half-mile across a field to Rolla and Dollie Neal's home to visit Dollie. Early in the afternoon, Doug went back home while Emma stayed with Dollie. Not long after Doug got home, it began to get stormy, and then the tornado roared through. The tornado completely destroyed his home and killed him. As his home was destroyed, a car was blown into a tree in the woods just east of his place. Emma was lucky that she stayed with Dollie when the tornado roared through. Rolla and Dollie's home was near the northern edge of the tornado, and it only lost some of its windows. Because the home was not damaged much, Emma, Dollie, and Dollie's two-year-old son, Billy, were not injured at all. They did see a lot more damage south of their home and on the other side of the road. A wooded area had been badly damaged with quite a few uprooted trees, and an old log barn in the wooded area had been badly damaged.

During the day, Rolla had been working with team members on the Illinois Central Railroad track near Akin, and when he started home on his horse, he could see a big, black cloud coming toward him. He was trying to go home faster because it would likely start raining. However, as he was passing through Akin, he could tell that the big, black cloud was actually a large tornado and very dangerous. As he saw the tornado roaring by south and east of where he was, he was really worried that his home might have been destroyed and his wife and son killed. He hurried home, and he was pleased to find that his home had not been destroyed and his wife and son were okay. However, he could tell that many of the neighbors' homes nearby on Eastern Road were destroyed. He saw that, just east of his home, the Deat Akin's place had been almost completely destroyed. Deat's barn and most of his house had been blown away, and the only part of the house that was still standing was one of its rooms. Since Rolla and Dollie's home was in good shape, they decided to take their wagon out to pick up people who had been hurt in the nearby destroyed homes and bring them back to their home. They used the two front rooms in their home as a hospital for the injured people they found.

William (Billy) Neal shown next to the Deal Akin place in August of 2007. He was in his family's
home when its windows were blown out as the tornado came by in 1925.
(Photo Courtesy of William (Billy) Neal, and taken by Bob Johns)

The last two places the tornado hit in Eastern Township were Oris Shirley's farm and James Biddle's farm. Oris Shirley's home and barn were destroyed, and James Biddle's home was almost demolished. James Biddle was badly injured and died several months later. He was one of the seven people who died as a result of the tornado in rural Eastern Township. The tornado roared out of Franklin County at 3:12 p.m.

The James Biddle home badly damaged by the tornado. (Photo courtesy of "Nadine Braden" Broyles).

In Franklin County, at least 184 people were known to have died because of the tornado. In Six Mile Township, only two people were known to have died because the tornado stayed along Big Muddy River, where fewer people lived in this township. In the part of Denning Township west of West Frankfort, where more people lived, twenty-three people were known to have died. In the town of West Frankfort, where many people lived, approximately eighty people died. In the part of Frankfort Township northeast of West Frankfort, fifty-two people were known to have died, thirty-seven of who were in the Peabody Mine #18 village area. In Cave Township, twenty people were known to have died, nineteen of who were in Parrish. In Eastern Township, seven people were known to have died.

Devastation in Hamilton County, Illinois

It started out as a rather nice day in Hamilton County on March 18, 1925. However, no one knew that, shortly after noon, a tornado had formed a long way off in the Ozark Mountain region of southern Missouri. During the next three hours, the tornado roared across southeastern Missouri and southwestern Illinois. By the time it got across Franklin County and was about to enter Hamilton County, approximately 505 people had either been killed instantly or very badly injured and died later. It roared into Hamilton County at 3:12 p.m., and it was about one-mile wide. As it roared across Hamilton County, it caused devastation in the following townships: Flannigan, Twigg, Mayberry, and Crook.

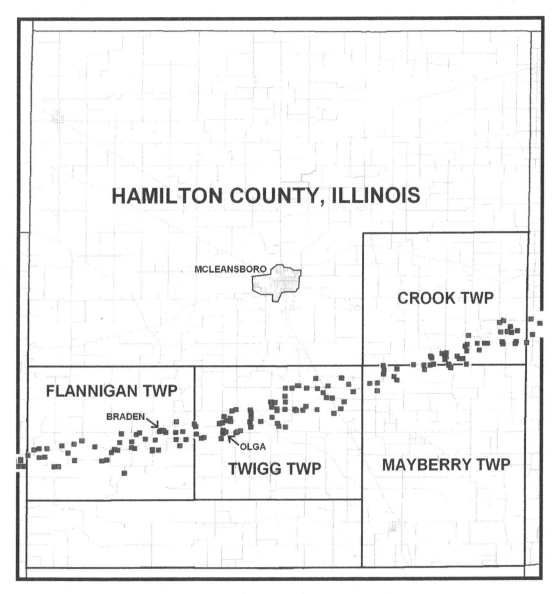

Black points that show where the 1925 Tri-State Tornado event was known to have caused damage as it roared across four townships in Hamilton County, Illinois.

Flannigan Township

From northwest of West Rural Hill to east of Braden

As the tornado started roaring into Flannigan Township, it badly damaged the Oak Grove Church that was along County Road 500N and just a few yards east of the Franklin-Hamilton County line. One of the first homes devastated in Flannigan Township was Miss Ollie Flannigan's home along County Road 500N. Ollie's home and barn were blown away, and she and her brother, Sam, were killed. The tornado blew away a photograph Ollie had on a mantle in her home, and it landed in Bone Gap, Illinois, fifty miles away to the northeast. Ollie's sister, Sissie Flannigan, lived in a home that was somewhere within a mile of Ollie's home. Sissie's home was also destroyed, and she was injured but not killed.

On the other side of the road from Ollie Flannigan's place and a little farther east, the tornado devastated Columbus Hick's place. Columbus's home and barn were destroyed, and he and his daughter-in-law, Martha Hicks, were killed. Down south on County Road 100E, the tornado badly damaged Joe French's home and outbuildings. Up north near the edge of the tornado path, some of the buildings on John W. Smith's farm along County Road 25E were only slightly damaged. Close by along County Road 525N, Henry Frazier's barn and henhouse were damaged a little bit, but fortunately, his home was fine. After the tornado occurred, he gave food and shelter to several neighbors whose homes had been badly damaged or destroyed.

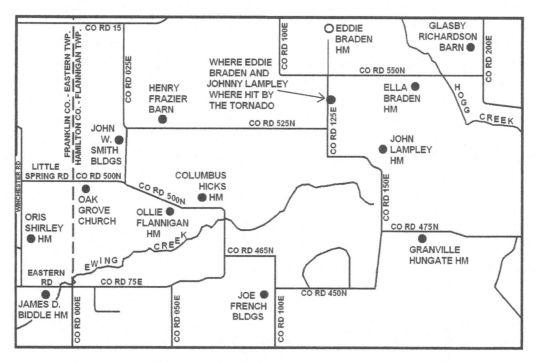

Black circle points that show tornado damage locations in western Flannigan Township, and near the Franklin-Hamilton County line. One white circle point shows where a home was not hit by the tornado and not damaged. On this and the rest of the Hamilton County damage location maps, more recent roads and what they are called are shown so you can tell where the 1925 tornado damage occurred. Also, a few of the roads that were there in 1925 and had been taken away sometime later, have been placed on these maps.

As the tornado roared farther into Flannigan Township, many more people experienced this terrible event. During the morning before the tornado occurred, Eddie Braden was at home with his wife, Lena, his eight-year-old son, Coy, his five-year-old daughter, Nadine, and his three-year-old daughter, Maxine. He and a neighbor, Johnny Lampley, had planned to go on a horseback riding trip that day to see some of their neighbors. He left on his horse around noon to meet with Johnny. After they got together and had been riding a while, they saw it was getting dark and a bad storm was coming from the west. They soon realized a tornado was coming rapidly toward them, and they decided to ride north on County Road 125E as fast as they could to get away from the tornado. However, they soon realized they could not make it away from the tornado. They stopped next to the road and laid down on the ground. As the tornado started to hit them, they both were able to hold on to the bottom of a tree next to them, and even though they were both blown off the ground, they were not blown away and not hurt.

After the tornado had gone by, they both got up and looked around. Johnny could see that his parents, John and Nancy Lampley, had their home blown away. He was really worried about them, and he quickly started back to their place. Eddie had also seen that John Lampley's home had been destroyed, but he was not able to see what happened to his family's home. He decided he should quickly go home to see if Lena and their children were all right. However, he could not find his horse, so he had to walk home as fast as he could.

As the storm was approaching Eddie Braden's home, Lena was inside with her children, and she was preparing fabric for some of her family's clothing. When the storm got closer, they started hearing a loud noise and saw very strong winds that really scared them. But fortunately, the noise died down after a little while, and the tornado seemed to be gone. It was still raining and windy, but Coy decided to go out onto their porch to see what happened. When he got out there, he did not see anything damaged, but he saw his father's horse. It seemed upset because it was running back and forth along their farm fence and was not able to get into their place. When his mother found out about the horse, she was really worried because Eddie was not riding it, and she wondered what might have happened to him. Because Eddie was running home, he got there soon and opened the gate so his horse could come in. When Lena and her children saw Eddie, they were really happy to see that he was in good shape. Eddie was also happy to find that their home was not destroyed and they were all right. He told them that he was really pleased to see that the tornado had hot hit their house. However, he was worried about what might have happened to his neighbors, including Johnny Lampley's parents. He decided he would walk over to where one of the closest neighbor's home was located and see if they were all right. However, as he tried to go outside and walk over there, it had started hailing, so he stayed home.

Sometime later that afternoon, Johnny Lampley came over to Eddie Braden's home. He told them that, on his parent's farm, the tornado had blown away their home and barn. After looking around on the ground near where the home had been, he found his father, John Lampley, and he was dead. His mother, Nancy Lampley, was still alive but very badly injured. He took her to a neighbor's home that had not been destroyed and planned to take her to a hospital tomorrow. He asked Eddie and Lena to go back to his parents' farm area with him to help him get things done and to help some neighbors if needed. Eddie and Lena were able to go with him after they found someone to take care of their children while they were gone. They were glad they were able to help him get some things done during the rest of the day. When it was getting dark that evening, Johnny took Eddie and Lena back home.

On the next day, Eddie and Lena took their children down to the John Lampley place to show them what happened. When Nadine Braden was looking at where the Lampley home had been blown away, she also noticed that the sidewalk had been torn off where it used to be and was laying farther away in the yard. As she walked around, she saw the well in the barnyard. As she looked down in the well, she did not see water, but she did see a rooster down there. When her parents heard what she saw, they gave her some corn to throw done there for the rooster to eat. They were all pleased that the tornado had not killed the rooster they found down there.

*John Lampley's farm where his home and barn where blown away by the tornado.
(Photo courtesy of McCoy Memorial Library)*

*"Nadine Braden" Broyles next to her home in McLeansboro on November of 2005. In 1925 she was in her father,
Eddie Braden's home as the tornado went by. (Photo courtesy of Matthew Gilmore)*

As the tornado roared by south of Eddie Braden's place and destroyed the John Lampley family's home and outbuildings, three other neighbors had some damage. Down south of the John Lampley place on County Road 475N was where Granville and Vinnie Hungate lived. As the tornado hit their really nice two-story home, it was blown around on its foundation and badly damaged but not destroyed. However, their nearby barn was destroyed. Fortunately, no one was hurt or killed there. Southeast of Eddie Braden's undamaged home along County Road 550N was Ella Braden's home. As the tornado came by the Ella Braden home, it was only slightly damaged because it was near the northern edge of the tornado. Over east of Eddie Braden's home was Glasby Richardson's one-hundred-and-sixty-acre farm. The Glasby Richardson home was north of the tornado as it went by, so it was not damaged. However, the tornado hit one of Glasby's barns on the southern side of his farm and destroyed it. Also, on this part of his farm, he lost a lot of hay bales and fencing.

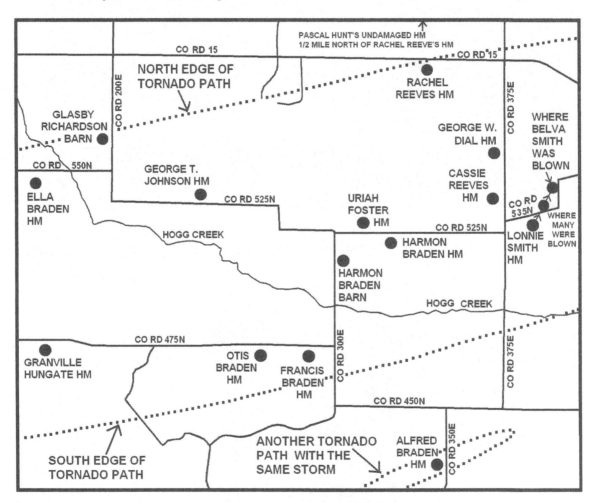

Black circle points that show tornado damage locations in the middle part of Flannigan Township. A line from one black circle point to another black circle point shows where a daughter got blown away from, and where she landed. This map has plat lines that show where the large tornado roared across this area and a small tornado occurred south of there.

As the tornado roared into the center part of Flannigan Township, many more places were damaged or destroyed. At George Johnson's farm on the northern side of County Road 525N, his home was badly damaged, and his silo was destroyed. About a half-mile south along County Road

475N, Otis and Ora Braden's home was very badly damaged, and their barn was destroyed. Just east of there was where Otis's parents, Francis and Betty Braden, lived and their home and barn were destroyed. Fortunately, none of these Bradens were hurt because they were away from their homes when the tornado came through. Otis and Ora were over at Roger's store in the town of Braden. However, since they did not have homes that were good enough to live in after the tornado came by, they had tents set up on their properties, and they were able to live in them until their homes were rebuilt.

Otis and Ora Braden's home badly damaged by the tornado. (Photo courtesy of "Nadine Braden" Broyles)

Up northeast of Otis and Ora Braden's home on County Road 525N, the tornado completely blew away Harmon and Pauline Braden's home and barn. Harmon and his two-year-old daughter, Ruby, were very badly injured. After the tornado moved away, Ruby could not be found for quite a while because, after she landed on the ground, a lot of trash had fallen on top of her. When she was found, they saw that her head had been cut open. So she and her father were both taken to a hospital since they were so badly injured. Fortunately, they recovered and left the hospital a few days later. Ruby had a plate put in her head, and she had to keep it on her for many years.

On the northern side of the road from Harmon Braden's home was where Uriah Foster had a very large farm. When the tornado came through his place, his home was damaged but not destroyed. However, across the rest of his farm, there was complete devastation. Four barns and other farm buildings were destroyed. At the barn that was destroyed next to his house, several of the cattle were killed. The tornado had injured Uriah someplace on his farm.

After the tornado caused devastation on Uriah Foster's farm and Harmon Braden's farm, it hit four more places as it roared east northeast across County Road 375E. On this day, Elsie Hunt and her classmates were dismissed from school early because the weather seemed to be getting bad. She was sent to her family's home, about a half-mile north of County Road 15 and Rachel Reeves's home. When Elsie got home, her parents, Pascal and Musette, were getting worried because they could see that the storm had many heavy clouds rolling around on the ground and causing damage. Before they got into their storm cellar, they stopped up above when they noticed that what they called the "big, bad storm" was passing by to the south of them and was not going to hit them. As they looked south as the tornado was going by, they could see all kinds of debris flying through the air. After the tornado had moved by, they could see that Rachel Reeves's home had been damaged and its roof had been blown off. They were worried about what happened to the Rachel Reeves's family and other neighbors who lived south of them. As it turned out, because the Rachel Reeves's home was near the northern edge of the tornado, it was not completely destroyed, and no one was hurt there.

On farther south along County Road 375E, three other homes were completely destroyed. About a half-mile southeast of the Rachel Reeves's home and on the western side of County Road 375E was where the George and Nancy Dial family lived. George, Nancy, and their children were at home when the tornado hit them. Their daughter, Helen, was really scared when she saw the tornado roaring toward her. Their home was picked up and blown down onto the road. Then it was picked up again, and when it was blown back down east of the road, it was torn apart and destroyed. Helen and some of her family members were injured, but fortunately, they were not killed.

On down south of George and Nancy Dial's place was a home that Cassie Reeves had rented. Her rented home was destroyed, but she was not known to have been injured. Just east-southeast of her rented home was where Lonnie Smith's farm was located. Lonnie, his wife, Lille, and their children, Belva, Roy, and Willie, and a neighbor, Sam Richardson, were all at his place when the tornado arrived. Lonnie and Lille Smith's home and barn were blown away to the north, and after passing over County Road 535N, they landed as debris up on the hill. All of the people in the home were also blown away. Belva was blown almost a quarter-mile to the northeast and landed in a tree next to the road, and she was wrapped onto a limb and killed. The other people blown northeast from Lonnie's home landed just across the road. Lonnie, Lillie, and Roy had been killed when they landed there. As Willie was blown away, his head was hit, and he lost one of his eyes and was badly injured. Sam Richardson was also badly hurt when he was blown away. When some people came to check on the Smiths, they found that some of those who had been killed had landed in a hog lot and some of the hogs were eating them. So they had to pull the dead people out of the hog lot. They also found that Willie and Sam were badly injured, so they picked them up and took them to a hospital.

Where Lonnie Smith's home and barn in the form of debris had landed in a hill area on the north part of his farm.
The debris had been blown north-northeast and had landed after it passed over County Road 535.
(Photo courtesy of McCoy Memorial Library).

On County Road 350E, south of the main tornado's path, is where the Alfred and Sarah Braden family lived. As the storm was approaching his place, Alfred noticed it was getting dark and windy and a roaring noise was getting louder, but he could not see the storm due to the trees around their house. He decided to get his children together and have his family go over to a neighbor's house. When they got together outside and took off going south across the field toward Willie Hine's place, they had not gotten too far when they looked back and saw a couple of their cows and pieces of their house flying up into the air. They were really scared and started running. By the time they got to Willie Hine's place, the loud noise and the flying debris were gone so they realized they were now safe. They decided to stay at Willie's home because their home was destroyed. A brief "little sister tornado" had destroyed Alfred Braden's home south of the main tornado.

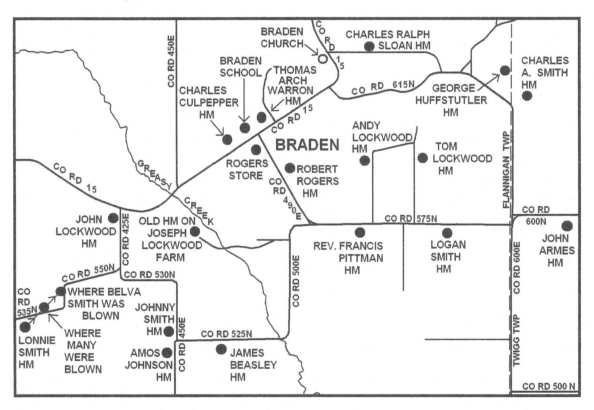

Black circle points that show tornado damage locations in the eastern part of Flannigan Township, the town of Braden, and the western edge of Twipp Township. A line from one black circle point to another black circle point shows where a daughter got blown away from, and where she landed. One white circle point shows where a church was not damaged by the tornado.

Back up north where the main tornado was roaring on toward the town of Braden, this devastating event affected many more people. Immediately after the tornado had devastated the Lonnie Smith place and killed most of the family members, it completely destroyed John Lockwood's home on County Road 425E. John and his wife, Eliza, were in their home when the tornado hit it, and as the house was torn to pieces, the debris fell on top of them instead of being blown away. After the tornado had gone away, some people came over and found John dead and Eliza badly injured under the debris. Farther east, John's son, Joseph Lockwood, had an old unused house on his forty-acre property that the tornado badly damaged, and the fences were blown away.

67

Down south on County Road 450E, Johnny Smith's home was destroyed, and he and his wife, Florida, were safe since they were ten miles to the northeast in McLeansboro when it happened. Just a few hundred yards south of Johnny's place, Amos Johnson, his wife, Artie, and their children were badly injured as his home was torn to pieces. East of Johnny's and Amos's home, James Beasley's home on County Road 525N was badly damaged, and the kitchen on the southern side of the house was blown away.

As the tornado roared into the small town of Braden, many of the buildings were damaged or destroyed. Charles Culpepper's home was the first building hit, and his home was badly damaged and almost destroyed. Just east of his place was the Braden School. The teacher, Lee Hunt, got worried as it was getting dark outside that afternoon, and he was hearing an increasingly loud noise. When he saw that some strong winds were starting to bend the trees over near the school, he had all of the students quickly move over to the center of the room and lay down under the seats. After they got there, a backboard and pieces of the chimney in the school started falling down. Then the school fell apart, and it was blown away. Lee and most of the students were blown all over the schoolyard, and some of the students were blown over on the southern side of County Road 15. Student Jean Braden was blown across the road and received a severe head injury. Jean was taken to a makeshift hospital that the Red Cross set up at the McCoy Library in McLeansboro. Fortunately, she was able to stay alive. Jean had a metal plate placed in her head to help her recover.

East of the school was Thomas "Arch" and Emma Warren's home. Emma was at home that day, and after it got dark and she heard the tornado coming, she looked out her west window. She saw it blowing the school down, and she was really worried because three of her children were in the school. As the tornado came on closer to her, she saw it pick up her buggy and blow it across her home. It landed in the field behind her home. Fortunately, her home was only slightly damaged when the tornado hit it. Emma noticed that it started hailing after the tornado had gone by, and when it finally ended, she ran over to the school area to find her children. She found them, and she realized her son, Jim, was badly injured. Because her home was still standing and not damaged much, she took her children and many of the other students over there. She helped care for the other students until their parents could come and get them. When Arch got home, he helped care for the students as well. As Arch and Emma were checking on their children, they realized their son, Jim, was in such bad shape that he should be taken to a hospital. When the hospital was set up in the McCoy Library in McLeansboro, they took him up there. Fortunately, while at the hospital, he got better, and after a few days, he was able to go back home. For several days after the tornado had occurred, Arch and Emma noticed that their old foxhound female dog was not anywhere near their home. When she came home, Arch checked on her. He saw she had spots on her where her hair was shaved into her skin. He figured that metal roofing had blown into her when the tornado hit her in their yard and she was blown well away from their property.

Braden School destroyed in the town of Braden by the tornado. (Photo courtesy of McCoy Memorial Library).

Down south of the Braden School and on the western side of County Road 490E was where Robert Rogers had his store. Robert was working there, and several local people were in the store when the tornado hit. Although the store was moved off its foundation and damaged, it was not destroyed, and people sustained only minor injuries. A lean-to on the back of the store was blown away. Over on the eastern side of the road and farther south, Robert's home and barn were completely blown away. His wife, Missouri, was injured and stripped of clothes as she was blown out of the house and went through a barbed wire fence. The only thing left on the floor of their house was a piano.

Roger's store damaged in the town of Braden by the tornado. (Photo courtesy of Micki Faruzzi)

Charles "Ralph" and Janie Sloan and their young children, Geneva and Dwight, were at Robert's store when the tornado came through. After the storm had passed by, they returned home, which was on a hill northeast of town. As they got closer to their home, they noticed that the tornado had not damaged the Braden Church. When they got home, they found that their house was still standing with only slight damage. A window had been blown out of the front bedroom, and a fence around the garden had been blown down. They were lucky that their home was near the northern edge of the tornado where not much damage was done. However, south of their home, the damage was a lot worse. About a half-mile south of them, Andy Lockwood's home and other buildings were completely destroyed. On south of Andy's place and on the southern side of County Road 575N was Reverend Francis Marion Pittman's house and farm buildings he had rented from Ralph Sloan. The tornado completely destroyed Francis's house and farm buildings, and he was blown out into a ditch and killed. His son, Paul, was severely injured.

There were three more places in the eastern edge of Flannigan Township where homes and other buildings were damaged and destroyed. On the southern side of County Road 575N and east of Francis's house, the tornado destroyed Logan Smith's home and barn. Logan's wrist was broken. North of Logan's home, Tom Lockwood's log house, henhouse, and barn were destroyed. Northeast of Tom's place and next to the Flannigan-Twigg Township line was George Huffstutler's place. The tornado destroyed his home and some other buildings as it was moving out of Flannigan Township.

As the tornado roared across Flannigan Township and devastated many places, eleven people were killed, and many others were injured. Most of the damage was in rural areas, but there was damage in the town of Braden. The Braden School was the only school hit and destroyed in Flannigan Township. A church was also damaged in this township.

Twigg Township

From west of Olga to Ten Mile Creek

As the tornado roared into Twigg Township, it first destroyed Charles A. Smith's home and barn, which were next to the Flannigan-Twigg Township line. Charles's farm was up on the hill where County Road 600E starts to turn northwest into Flannigan Township. There was a big forest on this hill area, and the tornado blew over many of the trees on Charles's farm. About a half-mile south southeast of Charles's farm and next to County Road 600N, the tornado hit John Armes's place. John's home on the southern side of the road was badly damaged, and a house and a barn that he owned on the northern side of the road were badly damaged.

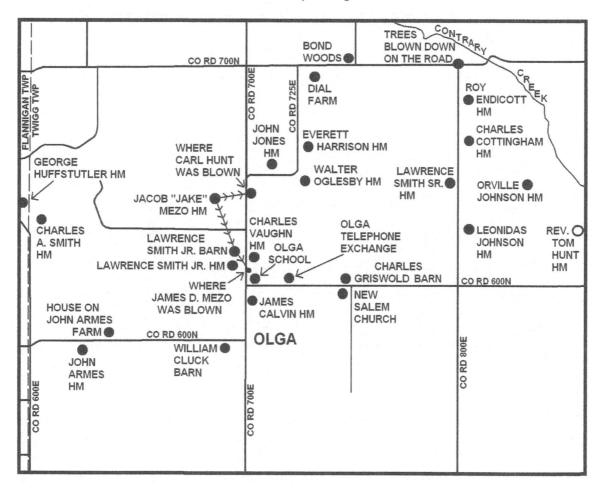

Black circle points that show tornado damage locations in the western part of Twigg Township and the eastern edge of Flannigan Township. Lines from one black circle point to two other black circle points show where two people were blown away from, and where they landed. One white circle point shows where a home was not damaged by the tornado.

Trees damaged by the tornado in a woods area on a hill of Charles Smith's farm (Photo courtesy of Micki Faruzzi)

John Armes's home damaged by the tornado. (Photo courtesy of Micki Faruzzi)

After the tornado entered the township and destroyed buildings on the farms of Charles Smith and John Armes, it caused devastation in many places as it roared on across County Road 700E and the Olga area. Along County Road 600N near Olga, William Cluck's barn was damaged. However, since his place was near the southern edge of the tornado as it was going by, William did not have his home or any other outbuildings damaged.

Farther north and up on a hill on the western side of County Road 700E was Jake and Effie Mezo's home. On this day, Effie's father, Reverend Tom Hunt, and her brother, Carl, came over to help Jake do some repair work on his barn. Also, Jake's son, James, came home from Olga School, and he was able to work with them. While they were working on the barn, they noticed it was getting dark outside and really getting stormy. So they all went outside and walked over to the south porch of the house where they could see what was going on. Effie was holding her five-year-old son, Thomas, in the house, and she also came out onto the south porch to see what was happening. They all saw what looked like a huge red ball on fire that was rolling around on the ground. It really worried them, so they all ran for cover in the house. Jake, James, and Carl ran over and made it into the western side of the house. Tom and Effie, with her young son, Thomas, started to go into the kitchen so they could get under the huge kitchen table.

However, as they opened the kitchen door, the tornado hit the house, and it was completely destroyed. The door fell onto Tom, and the chimney fell down onto the door and Effie. Thomas was blown out into the yard. Over on the western side of the house, Jake was blown down on the ground, and his shoulder was injured when a spike nail was blown into it. Both James and Carl were blown up into the air and well away from where they had been. As the tornado roared away, it started raining and hailing for a while. When it ended, Jake got up and started looking for the others. He found where Tom and Effie were trapped under the debris. He was able to lift the door and other things off Tom so he could get up. He was also able to get the large amount of debris off Effie and lift her up off the ground. Tom had not been injured, but Effie had been very badly hurt. After Jake found them and got them up, he and Tom started looking for their children. Jake found his young son, Thomas, down on the road south of where his house had been. Thomas was dazed and wandering around on the road. His face and body had been beaten badly, apparently by huge hailstones that had fallen on him, and his eyes were swollen together. Jake and Tom were really worried that they had not been able to find Carl and James anywhere near this place. When the tornado hit Carl, he was blown away more than an eighth of a mile to the east-northeast, and he was dropped down into a field next to County Road 700E. When the tornado hit James, he was blown away more than a quarter-mile south-southeast of the hill area. As he was dropping down some, he was about to hit the loft portion of Lawrence Smith Jr.'s barn, but just before he hit it, it was blown away, and he was blown through where it had been. He was miraculously dropped down to the ground, unhurt, next to the yard of the Olga School.

As James was being blown across Lawrence Smith Jr.'s farm, Lawrence's home was being wrecked. All but two of the rooms in his home were blown away, and the tornado blew Lawrence up into the air. He saw one of his cows in the air when he was there, and they both landed on the ground a long way from his house. Fortunately, he was not injured. When he got over to where his cow had landed, he found that it had been killed.

When the tornado hit Olga School, it was blown a few feet off its foundation and dropped partly down onto the ground. It was damaged but not destroyed. Fortunately, no one there was injured. Because the teacher could not get the door open, he and the bigger students helped the younger students get outside by lifting them through the windows. Then everyone was able to get out.

One of the school's students was Emmogene Mezo, James's sister. When she got out of the school, James saw her and ran over to tell her that their home had been destroyed. They both ran back to where the home had been to find their family members. Everyone there was alive, but their uncle, Carl, had not been found. They also saw that teenager Willie Oglesby had stopped by to see if his cousin, Effie, was okay. Soon, everyone found that Lawrence Smith Jr. was having injured neighbors brought over to the two-room part of his home that was still standing. Jake took Thomas down there, and Willie carried Effie down there. The next day, Jake, Effie, and Thomas were taken to the makeshift hospital that the Red Cross had set up in the McCoy Library in McLeansboro. Jake and Thomas were in good enough shape that they got out of the hospital after a few days. However, Effie was in worse shape, and she had to stay there for several weeks. Jake got a home in McLeansboro for his family to live in because their home near Olga was destroyed. Effie came over to their new home after she got out of the hospital. She was feeling much better, and a few years later, her daughter, Juanita, was born.

After the tornado and Willie Oglesby had already carried Effie over to Lawrence Smith Jr.'s two rooms, he decided to go home and see if his parents, Walter and Rella Oglesby, and other family members were okay. He started walking across fields to go home. As he was crossing over County Road 700E east of Jake Mezo's place, he saw Carl Hunt on the ground next to the road. He rushed over to pick him up, but he found that he was dead. He really felt bad about this, and he wondered if some of his family members had been killed. So he ran on across the fields to get to his home. As he got there, he saw that his family's home and all of their farm buildings had been completely destroyed. His grandfather, Frank Oglesby, who lived there, had been killed. His parents, Walter and Rella, were injured, and when it was possible, they were taken to the new hospital in the McCoy Library in McLeansboro. Rella was so badly injured that she was taken to the Missouri Baptist Hospital in St. Louis for further treatment when the hospital in the McCoy Library was closed.

In this area near and east of County Road 700E and between the Olga area and Country Road 700N, there were a lot more places were the tornado caused damage and destruction. Just east of where the Olga School was damaged along County Road 600N, the Olga Telephone Exchange building was damaged. A little farther east and on the southern side of the road was the New Salem Church where Reverend Tom Hunt was the minister. The church was blown off its foundation but only slightly damaged. On the northern side of the road near the church, Charles Griswold's barn had its roof blown off, and he lost his fencing. Along County Road 700E just south of the Olga School, James Calvin's home and barn were badly damaged. Along the same road just north of Olga School, Charlie Vaughn's home and barn were destroyed. Farther north and northwest of Walter Oglesby's place, John Jones's home and barn were destroyed. As the tornado hit John's farm, many of his cattle were blown away for a half-mile, and a few were killed.

North of Walter's place along County Road 725E is where Everett and Ruby Harrison lived. On the day of the tornado, they were working in their garden. When they saw the tornado coming, they both ran down into their storm cellar. The storm cellar door had a baling wire tied onto the inside of it, but they couldn't find anything to wrap the wire around. So Everett wrapped it around his hand so he could keep the door shut. As the tornado was getting there, it started to lift the door open and pull Everett out. The wire seemed like it was going to cut his hand. Ruby quickly got behind him and held on to him. Fortunately, they were able to keep the door and themselves from being sucked out of the storm cellar.

After the tornado moved away, they opened the door so they could come out. Outside, they found that their house and every other building on their farm had been completely blown away. North of Everett's farm, a house and some outbuildings were destroyed on the Dial farm. Northeast of the Dial farm and on the northern side of County Road 700N, the tornado uprooted and blew down many trees in the Bond Woods area.

After the mile-wide tornado caused a lot of devastation from the Olga area up to County Road 700N, it moved across County Road 800E and caused more destruction. At the intersection of County Roads 700N and 800E, many trees were blown down and blocked the road. South of there and on the eastern side of County Road 800E, Roy Endicott's house and barn were swept away. A little farther south, Charles Cottingham's house and barn were blown away. Farther south and on the western side of the road, Lawrence Smith Sr.'s house and barn were demolished. Farther south and on the eastern side of the road, Leonidas Johnson's house and barn were damaged but not destroyed. About a quarter-mile northeast of Leonidas's place was where Orville Johnson had his house badly damaged and his barn destroyed. About a half-mile east of Leonida's place is where Reverend Tom and Nancy Hunt's house was located. Tom's wife, Nancy, was there when the tornado went by. Their home was not damaged because it was near the southern edge of the tornado as it passed by. Although the tornado did not hit Nancy, her husband, Tom, and her son, Carl, were hit since they were at Jake Mezo's place when the tornado came by. Unfortunately, Carl was killed.

Lawrence Smith Sr.'s big home destroyed by the tornado. (Photo courtesy of Micki Faruzzi)

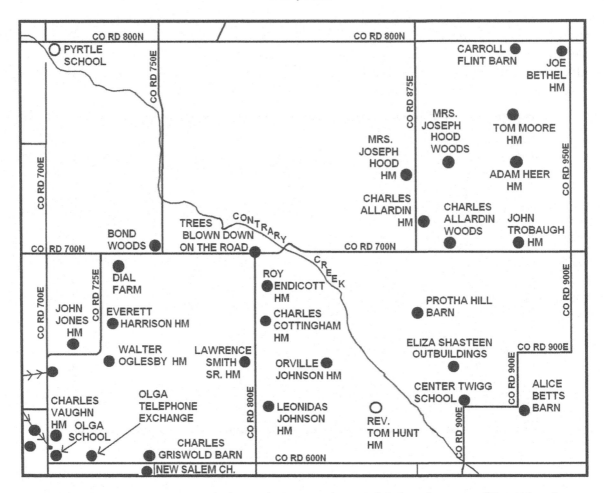

*Black circle points that show tornado damage locations in the central and northern part of Twigg Township.
Two white points show were some things were not damaged by the tornado.*

On the day of the tornado, Mark White was an eight-year-old student at Pyrtle School, two miles north of Olga School. Mark noticed it was really getting dark early in the afternoon. Because there was no electricity in the school, Mark had trouble reading because it was so dark. He looked out one of the windows and saw a storm was coming, and he could hear a lot of thunder. As the storm got closer and there was a very loud noise, teacher Thomas Warren told the students that a tornado was coming and they had to move away from the windows and stay in the middle of the room. Before Mark got over there, he looked out at the storm, and to him, it looked like a huge top turning around on the ground. While he and the others were sitting in the center of the room, it seemed very windy outside, and he could see some pieces of debris falling down next to the windows. After a few minutes, the tornado seemed to have passed by somewhere south of the school and was now moving away. As it was moving away, it started raining very hard and hailing.

When the rain and hail quit and the storm was gone, Thomas told the students that it was time for them to go home. Mark and his sister, Irene, left the school and started walking west on the road to get home, about a mile away. They soon noticed a lot of water in the ditches because of the heavy rain. As they walked up onto a high ridge, about a half-mile west of the church, they saw their dad, Floyd, coming toward them from their home. When he got to them he asked, "Was your school hit by the cyclone?" Irene said, "Nothing happened while we were there, and we were sent home." Floyd said, "It is good that you are coming home. Our home is in good shape. I think things were worse down south of your school" Because they were up on a high ridge, they looked down southeast and saw many houses and buildings they could usually see from up there were all gone. They went home, and Floyd was able to get a car and spend the next several days helping the people who the tornado hit south and east of them.

Mark White standing near his storm cellar in June of 2006. In 1925 Mark viewed the tornado going by from Pyrtle School (Photo courtesy of Mark White, and taken by Bob Johns)

As the mile-wide tornado roared on across Contrary Creek and into central Twigg Township, it hit Mrs. Joseph Hood's farm and Charles Allardin's farm along County Road 875E. Arminda Hood's home was blown off its foundation, and her barn was destroyed. In her wooded area on the eastern side of the road, many trees were uprooted, and the tree dirt mounds were still showing up many years later. Charles Allardin's home, barn, and outbuildings were completely destroyed, and two of the family members were injured. East of Charles's home and along County Road 700N, his woods had many of its trees blown down, and a lot of debris blown into the trees were still standing.

Up near the northern edge of the tornado path and on the southern side of County Road 800N, Carroll Flint's barn was destroyed. Farther east near the intersection of County Road's 800N and 950E, Joe Bethel's home had its roof blown off. Between Joe Bethel's home and County Road 700N, the tornado hit three other farms. Tom Moore's house and outbuildings were badly damaged. South of Tom's place, Adam Heer's house and barn were destroyed, and one of his stocks was killed. South of Adam's place and near County Road 700N, John Trobaugh's house and barn were also destroyed. John's wife and daughter were injured. On down south of County Road 700N, Protha Hill's barn was destroyed. Farther south, Eliza Shasteen's home, henhouse, and smokehouse were badly damaged. Forty-nine of her hens were killed. Along County Road 900E and near the southern edge of the tornado, the Center Twigg School was blown around on its foundation, but it was only slightly damaged. East of the school, Alice Betts's barn was demolished.

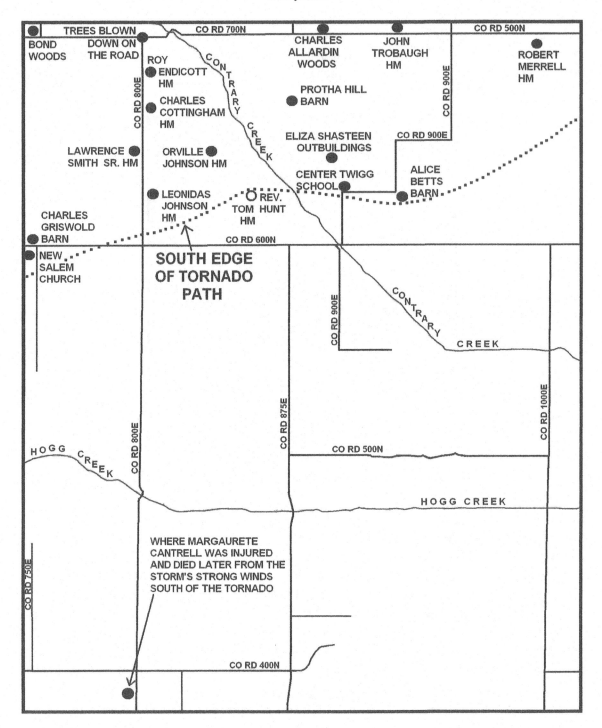

Black circle points that show damage locations in the central Twigg Township.
One white point shows were some things were not damaged by the tornado.

In 1925, Margarete Cantrell was a widow living with her youngest son, James "Jim" Cantrell, and his wife, Josie, and their children. On the day of the tornado, she, Jim, and Josie's daughter, Ciotha, were visiting her older son, Fayette "Fate" Cantrell, and his wife, Janie. Fate's home was near the southwestern side of the intersection of County Road 800E and County Road 400N. After visiting for a while, it was getting dark and stormy outside as a storm and its tornado were moving into Hamilton County. So this might have been why Margarete decided to go back to Jim's home and take Ciotha with her. Jim's home was on his farm, just south of Fate's place. As they started walking down there through fields and tree areas, the storm was taking the devastating tornado across County Road 800E, about two miles north of them. They were lucky that the tornado was not hitting them, but the storm was also producing some strong southerly winds down where they were walking. The strong winds were not as bad as the tornado, but some tree limbs and a few small trees were blown down where they were walking. As Margarete was crossing a barbed wire fence, her dress became caught. She was unbalanced from having her dress caught on the wire, and the strong southerly winds blew her backward, causing her to fall. Margarete fell onto one of the small trees that had been blown down. She became impaled upon one of the tree's stumps and was stabbed through her back. She was able to lift herself off the tree stump, and she went on home with Ciotha. Unfortunately, because of the way she was injured, she developed blood poisoning and died a few days later.

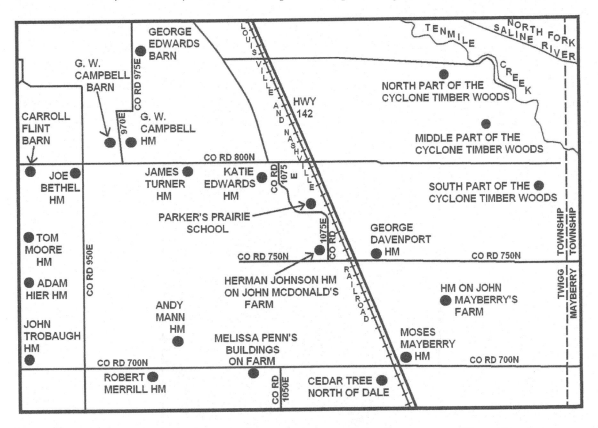

Black circle points that show tornado damage locations in the northeastern part of Twigg Township.

Back up north, where the tornado was roaring on to the east-northeast after it crossed over County Road 950E, a lot more damage and destruction occurred across the rest of Twigg Township. In this area, the tornado was almost a mile and a half wide, and near the northern edge of the tornado on County Road 975E, George Edwards's large barn had its roof blown off. Down farther south on County Road 970E, G.W. Campbell's home and barn was badly damaged. Southeast of G.W. Campbell's place and along County Road 800N, James Turner's home and barn were badly damaged. As the tornado hit James's place, two of his horses that were standing in his barn lot were blown up into the air and landed almost two miles away. Fortunately, they were not badly injured or killed.

On farther east along County Road 800N and near County Road 1075E, Katie Edwards's home and barn were destroyed.

On down southeast on County Road 1075E is where the Parker's Prairie School was located. On the day of the tornado, teacher Miss Clara Cook and more than a dozen students were in the school. As it got dark and stormy in the afternoon, Wesley Cluck decided to hurry over to the school and take his children home. As he got there, the tornado hit the school, and it was completely destroyed. Wesley was badly injured, and he died a few hours later. Twelve-year-old Earl Mayberry was blown into a tree, and he was killed. All of the other students, including Wesley's two sons, were injured. Clara was very badly injured with a broken hip and fractured arm.

Down south of the school, along County Road 1075E, was where Herman Johnson had a home and barn on John McDonald's farm. The tornado destroyed his home and barn and killed his stock.

On down near County Road 700N, near the southern edge of the tornado path, several places were damaged. On the southern side of the road, Robert Merrill's home and barn were badly damaged and almost destroyed. On the northern side of the road, Andy Mann's home was badly damaged, and his barn and henhouse were destroyed. East along the road, Melissa Penn had several buildings damaged on her farm, some on the southern side of the road and others on the northern side. Farther east along the road and north of the town of Dale is where the tornado blew a board into the northwestern side of a cedar tree. Over the years, the cedar tree has gotten much bigger, and in 2006, the board could still be seen in the tree.

A board that was blown into a cedar tree by the tornado in 1925 about a mile north-northwest of the town of Dale. And it was still there when this photo was taken in July of 2006. (Photo courtesy of Micki Faruzzi, and taken by Bob Johns)

As the tornado roared across the railroad, it hit Moses Mayberry's home on the northern side of County Road 700N and caused some damage. However, it was not badly hurt. No one was injured there, but Moses's son, Earl, was killed at Parker's Prairie School, and his other son, Wheller, was injured there. Northeast of Moses's place in the farm owned by John Mayberry, a house and some buildings were badly damaged. Just east of the railroad on County Road 750N, George Davenport's home was damaged, and his barn was destroyed. As the tornado roared over the wooded area on the western side of Ten Mile Creek, many trees were blown down, and some were uprooted. For many years after this occurred, the area was called the "Cyclone Timber Woods." As the tornado was roaring across the eastern part of Twigg Township, someplace in this area was where the tornado hit Walter and Nellie Mick. They were both badly injured, and Nellie died a few days later.

After the tornado crossed over Ten Mile Creek, it left Twigg Township and entered Mayberry Township. As the tornado roared across Twigg Township and devastated many places in rural areas and in the town of Olga, five people were either killed or badly injured and died later. Also, many other people were hurt. The storm producing the tornado also killed another person in Twigg Township with its strong winds on the southern side of the tornado. The tornado hit three schools in Twigg Township. One was destroyed, and the other two were damaged. Also, one church was damaged in this township.

Mayberry Township

From near Ten Mile Creek to near Lick Creek

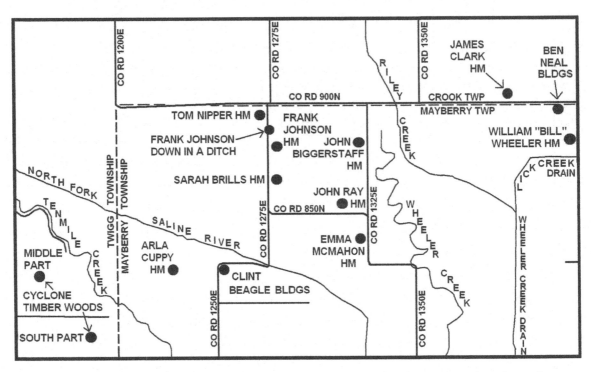

Black circle points that show tornado damage locations in the northeast edge of Twigg Township, the northwestern part of Mayberry Township, and on the southwest edge of the Crook Township.

When the tornado roared across Ten Mile Creek, and got into the northwestern part of Mayberry Township, it hit Arla Cuppy's farm, and his house and other buildings were destroyed. Directly east of his farm, there was lots of damage to buildings on a farm that Clint Beagle owned. Even though the tornado was only roaring across a small part of Mayberry Township, ten more family homes and buildings were either badly damaged or destroyed. Along County Road 1275E was where the tornado hit Tom Nipper's farm, Frank Johnson's farm, and Sarah Brills's place. On that day, Frank had gone over to Tom Nipper's place to help him fix some problems he had with his barn and the horse in there. As they were working on this and almost had it done, it started getting really dark outside, and they had trouble seeing what they were trying to do. It also started to sound noisy outside, so they looked out the window and could see a really bad storm coming. A lot of debris was flying in the air. Frank decided to run to his home, less than a quarter-mile south of Tom's place, and Tom ran over to his home so he could take his wife, Parthenia, and others down to their storm cellar. They made it into the storm cellar before the tornado arrived. However, after Frank began running home, he could tell that the tornado was going to hit him before he got to his destination. So he laid down in a ditch next to the road and hung on to a bush.

Down at Frank's home, his wife, Vesta, had earlier seen that it was getting dark outside, and she was worried that a bad storm might be coming. Because her aunt, Sarah Brills, lived in an old, small house down south of her, she knew that, if a really bad storm got there, it could easily tear up Sarah's home. So Vesta went down to Sarah's home, and as she got there, she could tell that a really bad storm was coming. She had Sarah and her daughter, Arrilla, go back with her to her home, and they made it just before the tornado got there. Vesta's home was a large, two-story place. She got in the middle of her home with Sarah and Arrilla, and she held her young son, Dean, with her.

As the tornado roared into this area, Tom Nipper's home was badly damaged, and his barn was blown away. Because Tom had gotten everyone at home down into his storm cellar before the tornado got there, no one was hurt. As Frank Johnson was lying down in the ditch and holding on to the bush, the tornado did not blow him away. However, he was injured and really felt sore for a while. Frank and Vesta Johnson's barn was destroyed, and their home was blown almost one hundred feet away from its foundation. Although it was not completely destroyed, two porches were blown off, and the chimneys and several of the windows were blown out. Fortunately, since Vesta had everyone in the middle of the house, no one was hurt. It was good that Vesta brought Sarah and Arrilla to her home because the tornado had completely destroyed Sarah's home and blew it away.

Less than a half-mile east of where Sarah's home was blown away, John Ray's home next to County Road 850N was also blown away, and John's wife, Minerva, was killed. South of John's place and along County Road 1325E, Emma McMahon's home and other buildings were badly damaged. Her home caught on fire after it was damaged, and it was completely burned away. North of her place along County Road 1325E, John Biggerstaff's home and barn were destroyed, and he was injured.

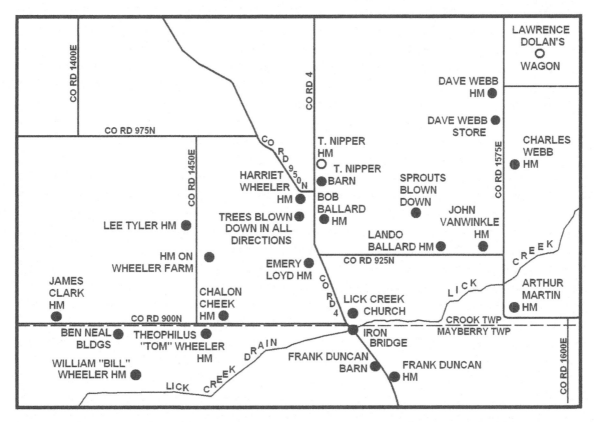

Black circle points that show tornado damage locations in north central Mayberry Township and south central Crook Township. Two white points show where some things were not damaged by the tornado.

As the tornado started roaring into the southern side of Crook Township, it was still causing damage and destruction on the northern edge of Mayberry Township. It swept away Ben Neal's house and barn next to County Road 900N. And down south-southeast of Ben Neal's farm, the tornado hit William "Bill" Wheeler's home, barn, and outbuildings and tore them to pieces. Bill was badly injured. A crosscut saw he had hanging up over the door in his log house was blown almost four hundred feet to the northeast. Part of it landed on one tree, and the other part of it landed in another tree. Northeast of Bill's farm and next to County Road 900N, Theophilus "Tom" Wheeler's home, henhouse, smokehouse, and barn were all destroyed, and one cow was killed.

By the time the tornado was reaching County Road 4, it was mostly in Crook Township, and the last buildings hit in Mayberry Township were Frank Duncan's home and barn, which were along that road and less than a quarter-mile south of the Mayberry-Crook Township line. On the western side of the road, Frank's barn was destroyed. But a little farther south and on the eastern side of the road, Frank's home was just a little bit damaged because it was on the southern edge of the tornado as it was going by. However, because Frank was out of his house when the tornado was going by, he was injured.

Just inside Mayberry Township near the Mayberry-Crook Township line, the tornado hit the iron bridge on County Road 4 that was over Lick Creek, and it was blown away. The bridge and Frank's barn are the last major items known to have been badly damaged and destroyed in Mayberry Township.

Even though the tornado only roared over a small part of Mayberry Township, quite a few homes were badly damaged and destroyed. One person was killed, and several others were injured.

Crook Township

From west of the Lick Creek Church to east of Dolan Lake

As the tornado started roaring into Crook Township, it blew away James Clark's home and barn that were next to County Road 900N and near Ben Neal's farm that the tornado hit in Mayberry Township on the southern side of the road. When James's home was blown away, he and his family member, Alma, were injured.

About a half-mile east of James's home on County Road 900N is where Chalon Cheek lived. On the day of the tornado, Chalon had left his home and went to a neighbor's home along County Road 4 in Mayberry Township and south of Frank Duncan's farm. While he was there, it got stormy. He and his neighbor went into the neighbor's porch and looked outside. They saw a large tornado was near them, and they could tell it was going to pass by just north of them. As it was getting close by, Chalon looked up at his home, about a mile to the northwest. He saw it get blown away, and he was really worried about what happened to his family members. After the tornado had gone away, he went back home as quickly as he could. When he got there, he saw that his barn had been blown away as well. As he looked around, he found that his wife, Janie, and his stepdaughter, Mina Tyler, had been killed. He also found that his brother, Charles, who lived there, had been badly injured. He was able to get Charles taken to a hospital, but he died a few days later. The tornado had killed everyone who was in Chalon's home when it was blown away. On County Road 1450E, north of where his home and barn had been, is where a home on the Wheeler farm was destroyed, and Lee Tyler's home was destroyed.

As the tornado roared on across County Road 4, the Lick Creek Church and many other places were completely destroyed. Also, quite a few people in this area were killed. The Levi Hook family members, who lived north of McLeansboro, were worried when they heard that a tornado had hit the area where they used to live in Crook Township. In late December, three months before the tornado occurred, they had moved away from their home, about a quarter-mile north of the Lick Creek Church and along County Road 4. In early January, the Bob Ballard family moved into their former home down there. Levi decided to go there the next day after the tornado to see what had happened. He had his family get onto their wagon, and their horses started pulling them down there.

As they were traveling, his teenage son, Eli, wondered what they would find because of all the debris he had found where he was up north of McLeansboro. He was at Mason School on the day of the tornado, seven and a half miles north of where the tornado would pass by. In the afternoon, he noticed it was getting very dark outside. He went out into the school porch, and he saw it was hailing for a little while. Then it started raining hard and coming down in sheets. While it was raining, he saw something fall down onto the road next to the school. When it was raining less, he went out and picked up what had fallen. He found a type of leaf that sets over a sewing machine. After he brought it into the school, the teacher told him and the other students that it was time to go home. As Eli started walking home, he saw dishrags, washrags, shirts, underwear, and other kinds of clothes and debris that had fallen down all over the area. He wondered where all these things had come from. When he later learned that a tornado had caused damage down where he used to live, he realized that many of the things down there had probably been blown away.

As the Levi Hook family wagon was being pulled along County Road 950N and was on a hill, just before reaching the Lick Creek area, Eli looked southeast. Everything he was able to see below the hill in the Lick Creek area looked flat. Nothing was standing. As they got down near the bottom of the hill and were getting closer to County Road 4, Eli saw that the widow, Harriet Wheeler, had lost her log home. The torn-up pieces of her home were all on the ground where her home had been. He noticed that the trees north of where her home had been were still standing. However, in the wooded area south of her home, he saw that all the trees had been blown down in all directions, and many were uprooted.

When they got to the intersection of County Roads 950N and 4, Eli looked over to the northeast and saw that T. Nipper's barn had been completely destroyed and every part of the torn-up barn had been blown well away from where the structure had been. A few hundred feet north of where the barn had been, Eli could see that T. Nipper's home had not been damaged. He realized it had been north of the tornado path. As the wagon was being pulled south on County Road 4 toward their former home where the Bob Ballard family lived, Eli could tell that there was complete destruction on their farm where they had lived a few months ago. He could see that the house, barn, and outbuildings were all destroyed. When Levi got the wagon near where the Bob Ballard home had been, he stopped. Then everyone got off the wagon to check on what had happened in the farm area. Because they did not see any destroyed pieces of the house there, they realized it had been blown away. The only thing still there was the basement, and it had not been damaged or blown away. Because it was a safe place, they hoped the Ballards had been in there when the tornado came by. After they looked around for a while on their farm, they found where the house had been blown. It had first been blown down south about six hundred feet. They found two places along this path where the house appeared to have hit the ground because they saw north-south V-shaped holes in the ground where dirt had been torn off. Close to where the home had quit going south, they saw this large log still standing on the ground and some pieces of the house near there had been broken off. They realized that the house was destroyed in this area, but they only found a few pieces of the house farther south. Most of the torn-up pieces of the house were farther east on their farm. So after the house was blown down south for six-hundred-feet and then destroyed, most of the torn-up pieces of the house were blown off to the east and landed on one of their farm's fields. In this field area, is where someone else earlier found were Bob Ballard's wife, Edna, and their two young daughters, Vonna May and Lottie Jane, had been blown. Most of their clothes have been blown off them, and they had been killed. However, Bob was not found there since he was not at home when the tornado hit.

While Levi Hooks's family members were still out looking at the damage on the eastern part of their farm, Eli saw that, on the hill, almost every one of their sassafras and persimmon sprouts had been peeled and were down on the ground. While Eli was on the hill, he looked down southeast near the County Road 925N and saw that the home of Bob Ballard's parents, Lando and Mary Ballard, had been completely blown away. He would later find out that Mary and her parents who lived with her, Robert and Martha Adams, had been killed. Lando and his daughter, Maggie, had been badly injured, and they were taken to a hospital.

*Eli Hooks standing next to County Road 4 near Lick Creek Church in June of 2006. Viewing to the north behind
him, one can see how the area looks where Eli Hooks came down after the tornado occurred in 1925, and found
that his family's former home that Bob Ballard's family lived in had been blown away.
(Photo courtesy of Eli Hooks, and taken by Bob Johns).*

After they finished checking on what happened at their farm, Levi Hooks got everyone on the
wagon, and they decided to go south on County Road 4 and find out what happened to the Lick
Creek Church. As they started down there, Eli saw that Emery Loyd's home, barn, and outbuildings
on the western side of the road had been blown away. He would later learn that Emery, who was at
home when it was destroyed, was killed. When Levi got the wagon closer to the Lick Creek Church,
they could see that the church had been destroyed. Levi stopped next to where the church had been,
and everyone got off the wagon to check on what had happened in the church area. Before the
tornado had hit it, the church had been setting east and west with its front door on the western side
of the church. Eli could tell that most of the church had been blown away. He saw that the church's
north wall was lying on its side just north of where the church had been. When he got over there,
he saw it had eight windows in it, and two of the windowpanes were broken. He walked over to see
what the steps looked like, the ones that were next to where the front door of the church had been.
He saw that the six-feet-wide concrete slab had two parts of it blown off. He wondered how far away
most parts of the church had been blown. He walked around to see where they were but could not
find them. He realized they had to have been blown a long way off from this area.

While he was walking around to find them, he saw the County Road 4 iron bridge over Lick
Creek had been blown away. He found that the bridge had been moved about four hundred feet
east-northeast along the creek and landed crossways on the creek. When Eli got back near the church,
Levi decided to take his family back to their new home north of McLeansboro. They had found that
the tornado was very devastating in the area where they used to live. And they would soon find out
that seven people were killed in and next to their farm.

Lick Creek Church destroyed by the tornado. (Photo courtesy of Micki Faruzzi)

Eli Hooks at the Lick Creek Church area in June of 2006. When he was down checking on this church after the tornado had gone by in 1925, he found that it had been blown away. So, the church on this picture was a rebuilt church. (Photo courtesy of Eli Hooks, and taken by Bob Johns)

More devastation and some more people were killed when the tornado roared across County Road 1575E. On John William Mayberry's farm, the house where tenant Arthur Martin lived next to County Road 1575E and the Crook-Mayberry Township line was badly damaged. A barn and some outbuildings were blown away. Up farther north on the western side of County Road 1575E and next to County Road 925N is where John Raymond VanWinkle, his wife, Malinda, and their children lived. Malinda's parents, Lando and Mary Ballard, lived just west of them, and her brother, Bob Ballard, and his family lived farther west. As the tornado was coming toward them that day and it was getting stormy, Malinda was holding the door closed so her six-year-old daughter, Veda, and her one-year-old son, Johnny, would not go outside. Just after the tornado blew away Bob Ballard's home and killed his wife and two kids and also blew away Lando Ballard's home and killed Malinda's mother and grandparents, it then hit John Raymond and Malinda's home. The home and barn were blown to the north and completely destroyed. John Raymond was killed. Malinda's daughter, Veda, was blown into a ditch, well away from where their home had been.

Sometime after the tornado was gone, a person who had come over to this area to help people found Veda. To this person, Veda appeared to have been killed, so she was placed on a board. Veda and her dead father, who also had been found, were both taken to Dave Webb's nearby home, which had not been destroyed. Other neighbors who were killed or injured were also taken over there.

Up further north and on the eastern side of County Road 1575E is where Charles Webb's family lived. Charles's son, Elvis, was in their two-story barn when the tornado was roaring toward their farm. Elvis started running back to their home when he heard the tornado coming. But just as he got to the gate near the smokehouse, the tornado had arrived, and the smokehouse was blown away. Elvis was knocked down between two stones on the ground, and he held on to them. The strong winds tried to blow him back up above the ground. But since he was holding on to the stones, he was able to stay down. However, he was injured when debris hit him.

After the tornado was gone, he was able to get up. He saw that their home, two-story barn, and all of their other buildings had been blown away. He looked around to see if anyone else had been hurt. Two mules had been in the barn when the tornado destroyed it, and they were now nearby and did not seem to be hurt. As he continued looking around, he found his mother, Merica. He could tell that she had been killed, and that really made him feel bad. He picked her up and carried her over to his brother's home. The home of his brother, Dave Webb, had not been destroyed.

Dave Webb had his home and a store on his farm, north of Charles Webb's place and on a hill that was on the western side of County Road 1575E. His store was south of this home. When the tornado hit, the store was blown off its foundation and badly damaged. His barn that was near there was destroyed. However, his home was near the northern edge of the tornado as it came by, and it was only slightly damaged. Because it was in good shape, Dave had local people who had been killed or badly injured brought over to his home. Well more than a dozen people were taken over there, including Dave's mother, Merica, who had been killed, John Raymond VanWinkle, who had been killed, and his young daughter, Veda, who also appeared to have been killed. A person who came over to Dave's home was checking on these people. As the person was checking on Veda, who had been there for several hours, groans were heard coming from her. So she was found to be alive instead of dead. Her hip and collarbone were broken. Once the Red Cross set up the hospital at the McCoy Library in McLeansboro, she and the other badly injured people were taken over there.

On the day of the tornado, up north of Dave Webb's home and on the eastern side of County Road 1575E, Lawrence Dolan was out on one of his fields spreading hay for his cattle. He saw a bad storm was coming and decided to go back home on his wagon. On his way, he saw a tornado roaring toward him, and he knew he was not going to make it home before it got there. So he stopped and laid down in the wagon and held on to both sides of the wagon bed. As the tornado came by just south of him, he could see grass and weeds from his field blowing up over him, but fortunately, his wagon and his home farther north were not damaged.

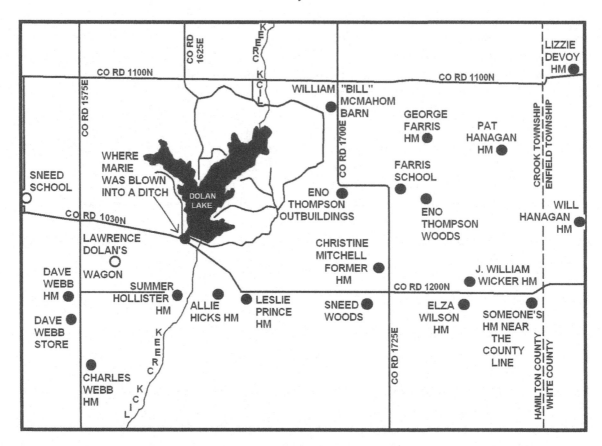

Black circle points that show tornado damage locations in southeastern Crook Township, and near the Hamilton-White County line. Two white points show where some things were not damaged by the tornado.

East of Dave Webb's home and near Lick Creek is where Summer and Rosetta Hollister's home was located. On the day of the tornado, Media Forester, Rosetta's married daughter, was visiting her mother because she was pregnant and about to have a baby. She had left the home where she and her husband lived in St. Louis a few days before and came over on a train to get there. Most of Rosetta's younger children were in the Sneed School on this day, but her daughter, Marie, did not go to school. In the early afternoon before it got stormy, Marie left her family's home and walked over to Leslie and Verna Prince's home to see their new baby, Charles. After Verna had shown her their new baby, Marie decided to walk over toward Sneed School to meet with the students who were coming home from school. However, as she was walking along County Road 1030N, she noticed a bad storm was coming. As she was going across the Dolan's property, the tornado was coming by, and even though she was almost north of the tornado path, she was blown off the road. She fell down into a ditch, and she was badly hurt. When the Dolan family members were checking on what happened to their farm, they found Marie and took care of her until the morning of the next day when they were able to take her over to the hospital that the Red Cross was setting up at the McCoy Library in McLeansboro. Marie was the first injured person who was taken there.

When the tornado hit Marie, it completely destroyed her family's home south of where she was. Summer, Rosetta, and Media were there when this happened, and as the home was blown away, they were blown into Lick Creek just east of their home. Rosetta and Media had been killed when they landed. Summer was not killed when he landed. However, because he was underwater in the creek and he was so badly injured that he was unable to get out of the water, he drowned.

90

On east of where Summer and Rosetta's home had been, the tornado completely demolished Allie Hicks's home and barn. The large, torn-up pieces of Allie's house fell down on top of him, and he felt he was going to die. However, an additional strong wind came along and moved the pieces of the house up off him for just enough time that he was able to crawl out to a safer area. So Allie was able to stay alive.

A little farther east of Allie's farm was the location of Leslie and Verna Prince's home and barn on Jake Heffner's farm. Marie had gone over there earlier to see Verna's new baby, Charles. When the tornado hit this area, Verna and Charles were still there. Their barn was destroyed, and their home was badly damaged but not completely demolished. Unfortunately, Verna and her baby, Charles, were in the part of their home that was damaged the most. Verna was badly injured, and Charles was killed. When Verna was found, she was taken to a hospital.

On farther east near County Road 1725E, the tornado hit Mr. Sneed's woods, and most of the timber was destroyed. Just north of there on the western side of County Road 1725E is where the house and barn on Christine Mitchell's farm were destroyed. Christine's husband, Michael, had died in 1923, so after that, she moved over to live in St. Louis, Missouri. One or more of her older children still lived on her farm when the tornado occurred, but no one was injured.

Up farther north near County Road 1700E, the tornado badly damaged two of Eno Thompson's outbuildings, his smokehouse and henhouse. About a half-mile east of where Eno's outbuildings were damaged, his woods had almost all of its trees blown down with some of them uprooted.

Next to his woods and along County Road 1725E was the Farris School. As the tornado came by, the porch was blown off the school, but the rest of the school was not damaged. So no students who were still at the school were injured. North of Eno's damaged outbuildings along County Road 1700E and near the northern edge of the tornado path, William "Bill" McMahon had his barn blown off its foundation, and it was only slightly damaged. That was the only damage he had at his place. At George Farris's farm north of the Farris School, his home had its roof blown off, and his barn and his fruit trees were destroyed.

The mile-wide tornado was about to move out of Hamilton County, but on the eastern edge of Crook Township, it continued to cause some major devastation. As the tornado was approaching Pat Hanagan's home, his wife, Barbra, and her two daughters were doing some spring-cleaning in their kitchen. As they heard the noise of the tornado as it was about to hit their place, they were really scared, and they held on to each other. After the tornado was gone, one of the daughters decided to open the kitchen door so they could go into the dining room. But as she opened the door, they could see that the rest of the house had been blown away. This really worried them. As they walked out to see what else happened, they noticed that their barn and outbuildings were all gone. They realized they were very lucky to have been in the kitchen of their house because it was the only thing still left standing.

Down south of Pat Hanagan's place and on the northern side of County Road 1200N was William Wicker's home. The tornado completely destroyed it, and his wife was badly injured and taken to a hospital.

On the southern side of the road was Elza Wilson's farm. Elza, his wife, Turza, and several of their children were at his place when the tornado was coming. Thomas McMurtry was also there on this day because he was visiting his daughter who lived in this area. They could tell it was getting dark to the west of them, and they thought a storm might be coming. However, because many trees were on the western side of his home, they could not tell a tornado was coming. But it was coming quickly toward his place, and Elza got worried when he saw some clouds moving around and he started to hear a roaring sound. He had everyone get inside his home. Just after they got inside, the tornado was arriving. They saw their wagon out on the driveway get blown up into the air, and then the home windows started breaking with the glass falling into the house. Then the tornado completely destroyed and blew away his home, barn, and outbuildings. As the destruction occurred, all were badly affected. Elza had a part of his hip joint broken. Turza was blown onto the ground, and a piece of the home's wall fell on her. When Elza found her, he was able to lift the piece of the wall off her and lift her up off the ground. She was badly injured but had not been killed.

Elza looked around their house area to find their children. However, he was not able to find their baby daughter, Edna Fern, and their son, Clarence, where the home had been. When he looked just northeast of where the house had been, he found both of them on the ground. A part of the wall from the house had also fallen on Edna Fern, and she had been killed. Clarence had been very badly injured. His head had been cracked, and some of his bones had been broken. He was in such bad shape that he was unconscious. Elza also wondered what had happened to his friend, Thomas McMurtry, because he could not find him.

After the tornado was gone, some neighbors who lived father south and were not hit came over to find out what happened and help their neighbors. When they got to Elza's place, they found that most of the Elza Wilson family was in bad shape and Edna Fern had been killed. As they looked around on Elza's farm, they found that Thomas McMurtry had been blown into the woods. A tree had fallen on him and killed him. Once they found everyone there that Elza knew about, they took them up to the town of Enfield in White County, where there were some doctors who could work on those who had not yet been killed. Clarence had a plate put on his head, and he was able to stay alive. Once they all got better, they decided to stay at a relative's home in Enfield because their farm home has been destroyed. Sometime later, Elza learned that, when the tornado had blown away his barn, the mules that had been tied up in the stalls of the barn had been found in a field about six-and-a-half miles northeast of where the barn had been. This place was northeast of Enfield in White County. The mules had not been hurt much, but they seemed to be scared. Some were still tied to the pole they had been tied to in the barn.

The last home that the tornado hit in Crook Township was someone's home east of Elza's farm and next to the Hamilton-White county line. A two-by-four was blown through its outside wall. It also went through another wall and landed on an outside porch. Fortunately, this board did not injure anyone, and because the home was near the southern edge of the tornado as it was going by, it did not have much more damage. The tornado roared out of Hamilton County at 3:36 p.m.

In Hamilton County, at least thirty-six people were known to have died because of the tornado and the storm with it. In Flannigan Township, eleven people were known to have died because of the tornado. They were in the rural areas. A lot of damage occurred in Braden, and some people were injured. But no one was killed there. A lot of damage occurred in Twigg Township. The tornado injured many people, and five were killed. Strong winds that the storm developed south of where the tornado had been injured one lady, and she died later. So the tornado and the storm had killed six people in Twigg Township. The tornado just crossed a small part of Mayberry Township, but several people were injured, and one person was killed. As the tornado roared across the rural part of Crook Township and devastated many places, eighteen people were either killed or died from it later, and many were injured. This township is where the most people in Hamilton County were killed, and it is where the tornado was even more devastating.

Devastation in White County, Illinois

It started out as a rather nice day in White County on March 18, 1925. However, no one knew that, shortly after noon, a tornado had formed a long way off in the Ozark Mountain region of southern Missouri. During the next three-and-a-half hours, the tornado roared across southeastern Missouri and most of southern Illinois. By the time it got across Hamilton County and was about to enter White County, approximately 540 people had either been killed instantly or very badly injured and died later. It roared into White County at 3:36 p.m., and it was more than a mile wide. As it roared across White County, it caused devastation in the following townships: Enfield, Carmi, Burnt Prairie (the southeastern edge), Hawthorne (the northwestern edge), and Phillips.

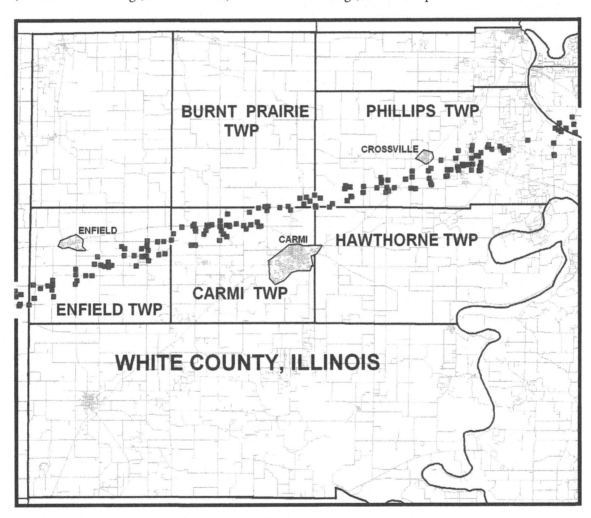

Black points that show where the 1925 Tri-State Tornado event was known to have caused damage as it roared across five townships in White County, Illinois.

Enfield Township

From south of St. Patrick's Church to southeast of Bethel Church

As the tornado started roaring into Enfield Township, it first hit William Hanagan's home and barn, which were up on a hill on the western side of County Road 25E. His barn was destroyed, and his home was blown away. William, his wife, Ellen, and their daughter, Kate, were at home when this happened. Ellen and Kate were blown out of their home area. Ellen landed on a tree, and she was badly injured. Kate landed on the ground, and she was very badly hurt with three of her ribs broken, a badly scratched face, and a big gash on her forehead. William was not blown out of the home area. He was found lying in a pool of blood, and he was badly hurt. William later looked for his animals and found that one horse and one hog were killed and two cows were badly injured.

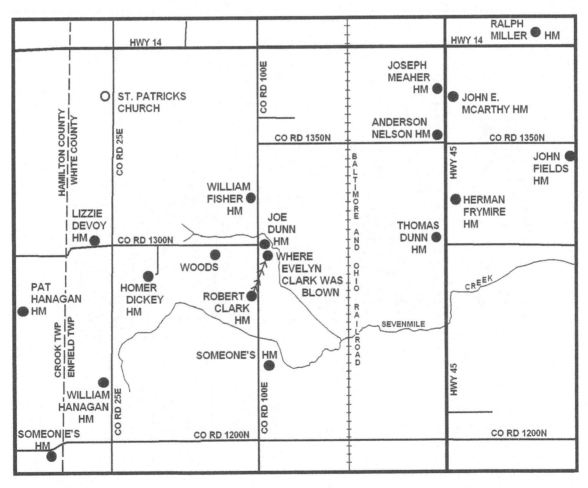

Black circle points that show tornado damage locations near the Hamilton-White County line and in southwestern Enfield Township. A line from one black circle point to another black circle point shows where a person was blown away from and landed. The white circle point shows a place that was not hit by the tornado and not damaged. On this and the rest of the White County damage location maps, more recent roads and what they are called are shown so you can tell where the 1925 tornado damage occurred. Also, a few of the roads that were there in 1925 and had been taken away sometime later, have been placed on these maps.

95

Up north on County Road 1300N and near the Hamilton-White County line was Lizzie Devoy's home. As the tornado was coming by, her home was near the northern edge of the tornado path. It did have a part of its roof blown off, but it was not destroyed. Lizzie and her two daughters who were there were not hurt. As the tornado roared on across County Road 25E and was about to hit Homer Dickey's place on the Sam Orr farm, he was in his new barn. His wife, Dessie, was in their home with her eight-year-old adopted daughter. Her daughter was in her bed since she was ill. As the tornado hit their home, it was moved a few feet off its foundation, and the roof was blown off. As this was happening, the daughter was scared because her bed seemed to be moving, and she asked her mother to come and get her. Dessie picked her up from the bed and started running through the hall to get into the kitchen. But as she was about to get there, she noticed that things were falling down in there. So she turned around to go to another room but stayed in the hall since her destination had already been torn away. Fortunately, it was best for them to stay in the hall area while the tornado was going by. Dessie did have one of her hands bruised, but she was not badly injured, and her daughter was not hurt. Homer was not injured when the tornado hit the new barn. The structure only lost a couple of its doors. However, the older barn that was close by was completely destroyed. So it was good that Homer was not in the older barn.

After the tornado was gone, Homer and Dessie checked on what else had happened to their place. They found thirty of their chickens killed in their yard. About thirty feet from the house, Dessie found a dishpan from her kitchen that had landed on a fence.

Homer Dickey's home damaged by the tornado. (Photo courtesy of the Libraries in Carmi)

East of Homer's farm and on the southern side of County Road 1300N was a wooded area that the tornado hit. Many trees were blown down. On to the eastern side of the intersection of County Roads 1300E and 100E was Joe Dunn's place. Joe was in Enfield when the tornado arrived, but his wife, Regina, was at home, and their two teenage sons, Francis and Isador, were working in one of the fields next to their small barn. As the tornado hit this place, the house was blown twenty feet off its foundation, and it was badly damaged with some of its rooms torn to pieces. When this occurred, Regina was badly injured with her left arm and right shoulder broken. When Francis and Isador saw the tornado coming, they ran over to the small barn and crawled down under it. Because they were able to do this, they were not injured. The small barn they were under was blown a few feet off its foundation and damaged. However, the big barn and three other outbuildings on their farm were destroyed. The smokehouse was torn up and blown against the side of their badly damaged house. Also in this area, some trees that were close together were uprooted and blown in different directions. Two horses and three cows were killed when the tornado hit him. Because Regina had been badly injured, she was taken to the Walker Hospital in Evansville, and while she was there, she was able to get in better shape.

Joe Dunn's home badly damaged by the tornado. (Photo courtesy of the Libraries in Carmi)

Besides hitting the Joe Dunn place along County Road 100E, the mile-wide tornado was known to hit three other places along County Road 100E. About a half-mile north of Joe Dunn's place and on the western side of the road, an unused house on William Fisher's farm was blown off its foundation. It was not badly damaged. However, about a quarter-mile south of Joe Dunn's place and on the western side of the road, the tornado completely destroyed Robert Clark's home on the Bailey farm. Robert was not at home when the tornado hit it, but his wife, Helen, and their five-year-old daughter, Evelyn, were there. As the home was torn to pieces, Helen was blown onto the stove. Her head was crushed, and she was killed. Evelyn was blown away from where the home had been, and after she was blown about a quarter-mile to the north-northeast, she landed near Joe Dunn's damaged home. Fortunately, she was not hurt much when she landed. More than a half-mile south of Joe Dunn's place and on the eastern side of the road, someone's home was damaged but not destroyed.

As the tornado roared on across Highway 45, five places were hit. Thomas Dunn's place was on the western side of the highway and near the intersection of an east-west road north of Seven Mile Creek. Thomas had his mother, Anna, his two brothers, John and Charles, and his two sisters, Maggie and Mamie, living with him, and they were all sitting together in the living room of their home. When the tornado hit their home, most of the rooms were torn off the house, but fortunately, the living room was not, and they were not injured. Thomas's Dodge car, which he had parked next to the home, was badly damaged with lots of things blown away. One of the tires was found a half-mile away. The new barn on the property was destroyed. Some of their sheep and hogs, as well as two hundred chickens, were killed. Thomas later found that one of their checks that was blown out of their house was found in Washington, Indiana, one hundred and forty miles away.

Thomas Dunn's home badly damaged by the tornado. (Photo courtesy of the Libraries in Carmi)

About a quarter-mile north of Thomas Dunn's place and on the eastern side of Highway 45 was Herman Frymire's place. On the day of the tornado, Herman, his wife, Beulah, and his father, John, were at their place. When they saw the tornado coming, they got into their yard and were lying flat on the ground and holding on to fence posts. As the tornado hit their place, their home and barns were completely blown away. John was blown loose from the fence, and he was badly injured. Unfortunately, he died a day later. Herman and Beulah were not injured much because they were able to keep holding on to the fence posts while the tornado caused the destruction at their place. After they got up and found that John was badly injured, they also found that two horses, one mule, three hogs, three sheep, and two lambs were killed on their farm. Their daughter was injured at the Trousdale School when the tornado hit it.

More than a quarter-mile north of Herman Frymire's place and on the northwestern side of the Highway 45 and County Road 1350N intersection was Anderson Nelson's place. As the tornado was coming, Anderson and his wife, Emma, were at home. Their home and barn were completely destroyed, and a number of trees in their yard were uprooted. After the tornado was gone, Anderson was sitting on his chair on the floor of their house that was still there, and he was rocking back and forth. He was so scared that he did not know what he was doing. Fortunately, he and Emma were unhurt.

About a quarter-mile north of Anderson Nelson's place and on the same side of Highway 45 was Joseph Meaher's place. On the day of the tornado, Joseph and his farm worker who lived there, William Devoy, were in his home. As they saw the tornado coming, they got into the storm cellar. And even though they were near the northern edge of the tornado, Joseph's home was badly damaged, trees were blown down, and the new barn was damaged. Also, three other barns on his farm were destroyed. So it was good that they got into the cellar and were not injured. Two horses, a cow, and two calves were in their barnyard when that barn was destroyed, but the animals were not hurt. A number of chickens were killed. Joseph noticed that eight of his beautiful big cedar trees in his yard were destroyed.

Next to Joseph Meaher's place and on the eastern side of Highway 45 was John Edward McArthy's bungalow home. On the day of the tornado, John and most of his family members were away from home when the tornado was coming. However, his twenty-one-year-old son, Glenn, was at home. And when Glenn saw the tornado was going to hit his house, he went into the basement. As the tornado hit his house, it was moved off its foundation and went across the yard. Then it fell down a hill and was demolished when it reached the bottom of the hill. As the house was moved off the basement, Glenn had a splinter driven into his lip. Fortunately, since he was in the basement, he was not badly injured. After the tornado was gone and he got out of the basement, he saw that the house and all the outbuildings had been destroyed. He also saw that their new car was badly damaged and the nearby farm fences were gone. One cow and about 125 chickens had been killed.

About three-quarters of a mile east of the Anderson Nelson place and on the southern side of County Road 1350N was John M. Field's place. As the tornado was about to hit John's home, no one was there. John was in Enfield, and his daughter, Harriet, and son, Willard, were at high school in Enfield. John's wife, Lisabell, and their two youngest children were at Alva Veatch's home, which was closer to Enfield than their home was. Fortunately, the tornado did not hit them since it was passing by south of them. However, two of their sons, eleven-year-old Edmond and fourteen-year-old John Jr., were at Trousdale School, which was northeast of John's place and on the northeastern side of the Highway 14 and County Road 300E intersection. Before the tornado got to the school, it hit John's place. Their house had its roof blown off, and the rest of the house was torn up on its foundation. Their barn was badly damaged, and two sheep and three lambs were killed. Just after the tornado tore up John's home and barn, it roared toward that school.

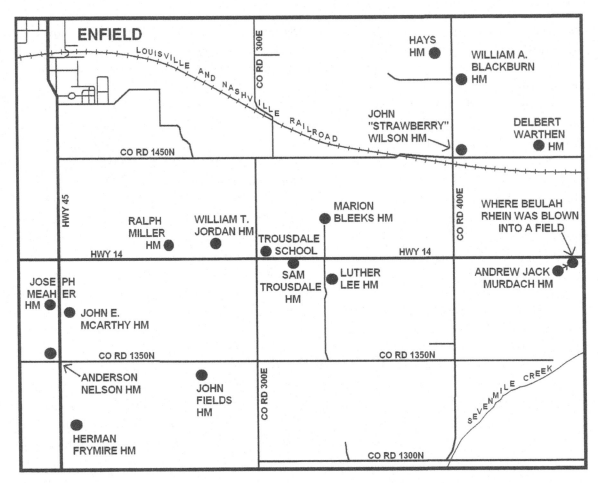

Black circle points that show tornado damage locations in the middle part of Enfield Township from south to east of the town of Enfield. A line from one black circle point to another black circle point on this map and the next map shows where a daughter got blown away from, and where she landed.

On the day of the tornado, teacher Miss Pauline McMurtry was at Trousdale School, and she had sixteen students. When the tornado hit the school, it was torn to pieces. The western side of the building came down on many of the students and then lifted off and went back west. As the destruction was occurring, Pauline was injured while she was trying to rescue some of the students. Something hit her on the left side of her face, and her eye was hurt. Also, her hip and legs were bruised. Even though Pauline was hurt, after the tornado was gone, she kept looking around to find the students. She found William Jordan's daughter, Reba, in a hole where a tree had been uprooted. Reba had been blown into mud and water, and if Pauline had not found her soon and gotten her out of there, she might have died. Her face was badly scratched and bruised, but she was able to stay alive. Pauline found Harry Erkman under the heater, so she pulled him out. He had not been hurt. As she continued checking on the rest of the students, she found that only two other students besides Harry Erkman had not been hurt. They were Fern Lee and Florence Malone. She found that Ralph Miller's twelve-year-old son, Vernon, had been killed. In addition to Reba Jordan, she found quite a few other students that were hurt. John Field's son, Jonnie, had his right leg broken in two places. His other son, Edmond, suffered a gash on his hip, and his head and face were bruised. Lee Jordan had some cuts on his head and one of his legs, but his injuries were not serious. However, Reba Hollister was very badly hurt. She suffered a fractured skull and bruises on her brain. Lucille Lee had a broken collarbone. Gilbert Veatch had a badly cut face and head. Roy Erkman had injuries inside his body. Charles Williams had been blown about a hundred feet from the school building. He had a broken kneecap, cut eye, and bruised face. Lee Jordan was cut on his head and leg, but his injuries were not as serious as many of the other students.

After Pauline found all of the students, she was able to have many of them taken over to one of the neighbor's homes that was not destroyed. Reba Hollister and some of the others were then taken to some place where they could get some treatment for their injuries.

The Trousdale School destroyed by the tornado. (Photo courtesy of the Libraries in Carmi)

The tornado damaged or destroyed most of the neighbors' homes near the Trousdale School. Sam Trousdale's home that was next to Highway 14 and about seven-hundred-feet east-southeast of the school was totally destroyed, and his wife, Bertha, was injured a little bit. His barn and silo were blown away. Marion Bleeks's home and barn that were about a quarter-mile northeast of the school were destroyed. Luther Lee's home and barn that were more than a quarter-mile southeast of the school were also destroyed. William T. Jordan's home that was about a quarter-mile west of the school was the only home near the school that was not completely destroyed. However, it was badly damaged, and William's barn was destroyed. Ralph Miller's home was about a half-mile west of the school, and it was near the northwestern edge of the tornado as it went by. So his home was only slightly damaged. However, his barn was destroyed. No one was injured at his place, but his son, Vernon, was killed at the school.

As the tornado roared across County Road 400E, the Hays's home on the western side of the road was destroyed, and it was near the northern edge of the tornado since there was no other damage north of it. Just south of it and on the eastern side of the road, William Blackburn's home was damaged but not completely destroyed. Farther south on the road and near its intersection with County Road 1450N is where John "Strawberry" Wilson's home was located. On the day of the tornado, John, who had been the president of Enfield High School, was at home with his wife, Mary Jane, and their two daughters, Rachel and Lucy. Mary and her two daughters were holding on to the hall door to keep it closed as the tornado was about to hit their home. However, as the tornado was hitting their home, the hall door blew open, and Mary and her daughters were blown out into their yard. Then most of their home was blown away. Mary and her daughters were badly injured but able to stay alive. After the tornado was gone, Mary noticed that fire had started on some of the debris where the home had been. She looked around to see where John was, and she found him down in some of the home debris. She pulled him out of the home area because of the fire that had started. However, once she got him out of there and checked on him, she found that he was already dead. The tornado also hit several of John's mules and horses on his farm. Two horses and one mule were badly injured, and another mule was killed.

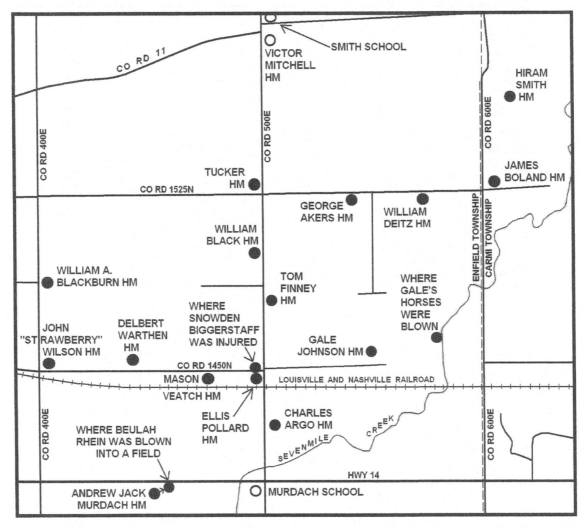

Black circle points that show tornado damage locations in the northeastern part of Enfield Township and near the Enfield-Carmi Township line. The three white circle points show where things were not hit by the tornado and were not damaged.

East on County Road 1450N from John "Strawberry" Wilson's place was Delbert Warthen's home. As the tornado was coming, Delbert, his wife, Maggie, and several of their children were at home, and Charles Argo was there visiting Delbert. The tornado completely destroyed Delbert's home, and everyone there were torn up. Delbert and Maggie's baby, Versa, and another baby were instantly killed. A two-by-four hit Charles Argo, and he was severely injured. Delbert was also severely hurt, and within a few days, both Charles and Delbert passed away. Maggie had both of her arms broken, and severe bruises covered her body. Her two-and-a-half-year-old son, Floyd, had a badly torn-up cheek, and all of his teeth were torn off. Her twelve-year-old son, Louis, had a part of his body torn open, and he suffered from pneumonia as a result of the exposure. Fortunately, even though they were badly injured, Maggie, Floyd, and Louis were able to stay alive.

On east of Delbert's place along the road, both Mason Veatch's home and Ellis Pollard's home were completely destroyed. Fortunately, no one was badly injured at these places. Ellis and Emma Pollard were visiting somewhere else when the tornado hit their home. When they returned home, the only things they could find where their home had been was Emma's sewing machine drawer and a piece of Ellis's underwear.

Down south of Delbert Warthen's place along Highway 14 is where Andrew "Jack" Murdach's home was located. On the day of the tornado, Jack's wife, Armintie, was at home, and her daughter, Ethel Rhein, was there with her husband, Alvin, and their new baby, Beulah. Jack's brother, Albert Murdach, who was blind and had been living in Jack's home for years, was also there. As the tornado hit his home, it was completely destroyed, and Armintie, Ethel, and Alvin were pushed down on the ground with much of the torn-up home debris falling on top of them. Armintie and Ethel were killed instantly, and Alvin was very badly injured and died a few days later. Beulah was blown out of the home area and landed in the brush on a field. Albert had gotten out of the house before the tornado destroyed it, and he laid down in the field as he heard the tornado coming by. Fortunately, he was not injured. After the tornado was gone and he had gotten up, he could not see what happened since he was blind. However, he realized there was damage around. Because he was in the field, he could hear Beulah crying. He walked over to where he heard her crying, and he realized who she was. He was able to pick her up and go somewhere where people could find them.

Even though Jake Murdach's home was destroyed, most of the homes and other buildings south and east of his home were not damaged at all since they were south of the tornado path. About a half-mile east of his home and near the intersection of Highway 14 and County Road 500E was the Murdach School, which the tornado did not hit.

During the early afternoon, teacher Snowden Biggerstaff noticed it was getting dark outside and a bad storm was coming toward their township. Because the weather looked bad, he dismissed his school and had his students go home. After the students had left and gotten home, he got on his horse and started going home near the town of Enfield. He had his horse go up north of County Road 500E, and after he got about a half-mile north of his school, he had his horse turn west on County Road 1450N. Just after his horse turned west and they were near the Ellis Polland home, the tornado hit them. They were blown off the road, and both were injured. Snowden had both of his arms and one of his legs broken, and he was down on the ground. His horse had a broken leg, but he was able to stay next to where Snowden was on the ground. When someone finally found them, Snowden was taken to a hospital in Evansville where his broken leg could be fixed. However, Snowden died while he was there.

Even though the Murdach School was far enough south on County Road 500E that it did not get hit, the tornado was more than a mile wide as it crossed this road farther north. About a quarter-mile north of the Murdach School was Charles Argo's home. When the tornado hit his home, his wife, Sarah, was there, and she was uninjured because their home was only slightly damaged. If Charles had been at his home instead of visiting Delbert Warthen when the tornado came by, he would have not been severely injured and died.

About a quarter-mile north of Charles Argo's place and on the western side of County Road 500E near the intersection of County Road 1450N is where Ellis Pollard's home was destroyed and the tornado hit Snowden Biggerstaff. More than a quarter-mile north of this intersection is where Tom Finney's home and farm buildings were located. When the tornado hit his place, his home and all of his outbuildings were completely destroyed. Tom, his wife, Clara, and their children, Mary, Clinton, and Helen, and Tom's farther, John, were all badly hurt. However, their children were more seriously injured. Mary had a bad scalp wound and a deep cut on the thigh. Clinton had his right arm broken and numerous cuts and bruises, and it was feared that his skull was fractured. Helen had a scalp injury and suffered from pneumonia from exposure. Everyone who was hurt at Tom's home was taken to the Blackburn home for treatment.

About a quarter-mile north of Tom's home and on the western side of County Road 500E is where William Black's two-story home and barn were located on the W.A. Smith farm. On the day of the tornado, William Richardson, a carpenter from Eldorado, was at this home visiting his sister, Sarah, William Black's wife. Sarah also had several of her children there. As the tornado hit William Black's home and barn, both were destroyed. William Richardson was killed. Some of the others there were injured, but they were not severely hurt.

Somewhere from northwest to south of William Black's home on the Smith farm's was where Mr. and Mrs. Miller Poore's home was located. Their home was badly damaged, and their barn was wrecked. However, no one there was injured.

About a quarter-mile north of William Black's place and on the northwestern edge of the intersection of County Roads 500E and 1525N was the Tucker home. It was blown off its foundation, but it was not damaged much since it was almost north of the tornado as it came by. The Tucker home was one-and-a-quarter mile north of where the southernmost damage along County Road 500E occurred at Charles Argo's home.

A mile north of the Tucker home is where the Smith School was located. On the day of the tornado, it began to get dark outside the school, and it looked like a rolling fogbank storm was coming. So the teacher took all of the students over to Victor and Edith Mitchell's home, just south of the school, where student Ruby Mitchell lived. Once they got there, they could see that the rolling fogbank had divided into tornado spirals and was passing by just south of them. Student Clinton Akers, George and Mary Akers's son, was standing at Victor's backdoor. And Victor was there with his daughter, Ruby. They were all looking down southeast as the tornado was hitting Clinton's family place on County Road 1525N, and they could see barn doors and other things from their place flying up into the air. When Clinton and his siblings from school got home, they found that their home, barn, and silo had been flattened onto the ground and chickens were running around without any feathers. Their brother, George Jr., who had been at home, was not injured much. However, their mother, Mary, had been badly hurt. Because the George Akers family had lost their house, they were taken to other places that evening. On the next day when Mary was staying at her son-in-law and daughter's home, she passed away.

After the tornado destroyed George Akers's home and buildings, the tornado hit two other places before it went out of the Enfield Township. Just east of George's place on County Road 1525N, the tornado hit William Deitz's place, completely destroying his home and barn. William was killed instantly. His wife, Ida, and their child were badly hurt.

Down south near the east end of County Road 1450N was where the tornado hit Gale Johnson's home on John Lamp's farm. As the tornado came by, Gale's home was badly damaged, but it was not completely destroyed. As this was happening, he looked outside and saw his two big horses turning over and over like balls. They were being rolled away to the east. After the tornado was gone, he went outside to find his horses. They had landed next to Seven Mile Creek. One had been killed, and the other was very badly hurt.

After the tornado destroyed William Deitz's home and blew Gale Johnson's horses next to Seven Mile Creek, it left Enfield Township and entered Carmi Township. As the tornado roared across Enfield Township, it stayed in a rural area and damaged or devastated more than thirty-two homes and destroyed Trousdale School. Fifteen people were either instantly killed or badly injured and died later. Also, many more people were injured.

Carmi Township

From near Seven Mile Creek in northwest Carmi Township to the northeastern edge of Carmi Township just west of Hadden School

As the tornado roared into Carmi Township, it first hit James Boland's home, which was next to the Enfield-Carmi Township line and on the northeastern side of the intersection of County Roads 1525N and 600E. As the tornado was coming, James and his mother, Rosa A. Smith, were there. His mother's last name had changed from Boland to Rippy to Smith since James was born. She was married two other times after James was born. James's sister, Lucy Ellen Phillips, who lived in Paris, Illinois, was at his place because she had come over to take care of Rosa, who was ill. She had also brought her baby over with her. When the tornado hit James's place, it completely destroyed his home and his barn. Rosa and Lucy were both killed. James and the baby were injured but not seriously hurt. About sixty of his chickens were killed and blown away.

On James Boland's large farm, Hiram and Irene Smith and their two-year-old daughter lived in a home that was almost a half-mile north of James's home and a little bit farther east in Carmi Township. Their home was destroyed. But fortunately, no one was badly injured or killed there.

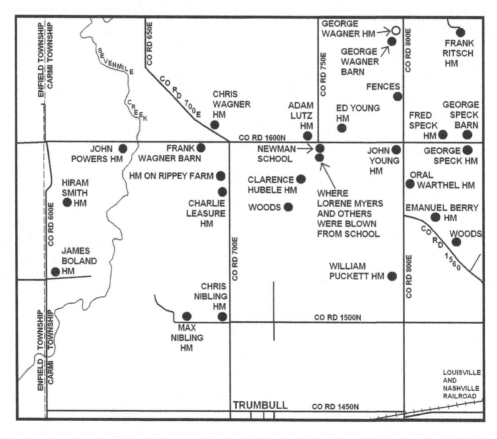

Black circle points that show tornado damage locations in northwestern Carmi Township. One of the black circle points shows where a student was blown from a school. One white circle point shows were a home was not hit by the tornado and was not damaged.

106

As the tornado was roaring toward Seven Mile Creek, it hit John and Nannie Powers's home that was just west of the creek near County Road 1600N. Their barn was destroyed, but their home was only slightly damaged, and no one was hurt there. After the tornado crossed the creek, it was still more than a mile wide, and it hit quite a few people's places by the time it roared over County Road 700E.

On County Road 1500N and up on a hill about a quarter-mile west of County Road 700E was Max Nibling's home. When the tornado hit his place, his home had a part of its roof blown off, and his barn and other outbuildings were destroyed. Fortunately, no one there was injured. On Max's farm and about a quarter-mile east of his home was where his son, Chris, had a home and barn. On the day of the tornado, Chris, and his wife, Pearl, were at home. With them were their young daughter, Alma, their little son, James, and their niece, Anna Carter. In the afternoon, it got very dark outside and very windy as the tornado was coming. Then their front door blew open. Chris tried to shut the door, but he couldn't because the wind was so strong. He asked his wife and children to help him shut the door. However, as they tried to help him, the tornado completely tore up their house and badly damaged their barn. Most were not badly hurt. But Pearl had her head cut, and she was seriously injured.

About three-quarters of a mile north of Chris Nibling's home and on the western side of County Road 700E was Charlie and Lula Leasure's home. They saw the tornado coming toward them, and they got away from their home as the tornado was about to hit. It completely destroyed their home and barn. However, they were not hurt because they had gotten away from their home.

About two-hundred yards north of the Leasure's home and also on the western side of County Road 700E was a home on the Rippey farm that was also destroyed. Northwest of the home on the Rippey farm and on the southern side of County Road 1600N was where the tornado hit Frank Wagner's place. Frank's barn and garage were destroyed, but his home was not damaged much at all. So he and his wife, Della, and their children were not hurt.

North of Frank's home and along County Road 700E is where his brother, Chris Wagner, had his home. Chris's home was more than a mile north of where the tornado hit Chris Nibling's home along County Road 700E. Because Chris Wagner's home was near the northern edge of the tornado as it was going by, the only damage he had on his home was a part of the roof that was lifted off. Because his home was only a little damaged, he and his wife, Clara, and their children were not hurt.

After the tornado moved on east of County Road 700E, it hit Clarence Hubele's home on a farm that Chauncey S. Conger owned at that time, and it blew away Clarence's home. Nearby, it also blew away a large barn and silo. Fortunately, Clarence and his wife were not at home when this occurred. Also, down south of Clarence's home and on Chauncey's farm was an eighteen-acre woods that had most of its trees blown down.

Newman School was next to the intersection of County Roads 1600N and 750E, and it was on the northern edge of Chauncey's farm. On the day of the tornado, teacher Jasper Mossberger noticed it was getting dark and stormy outside. So he went over on the western side of the school to look out one of the windows. While he was doing this, Lorene Myers, her brother, Charles, and the other students were sitting in their seats. Two doors were in the school building, but the door on the eastern side was nailed shut. So Jasper got to the other door on the western side of the building and held it shut because it was starting to get windy outside. He did not want the door to be blown open, and he did not want any of his twenty-four students to go outside. He looked back at the students while he was doing this and told them that a terrible storm was coming. Lorene and the other students jumped up from their seats and went over close to him. As the tornado started to hit their school, some plaster started falling from the ceiling on the southern side of the building. And as they saw the building walls starting to move in, Lorene and many others lost their memory as the school was being destroyed and the students and the teacher were being blown away. Lorene, Charles, and many of the others were blown down south into a field on Chauncey's farm.

When Lorene woke up, she noticed she was on the ground. It was raining, and hail was falling on her. She saw the long-shaped hail was really hurting her back and her legs. When her brother, Charles, woke up, he felt the hail falling on him, too. When the rain and hail quit and he got up, he saw the school's furnace rolling down the hill east of where the school had been. When Jasper got up, he realized he had been hurt, he had a bad cut on one of his legs, and he had bruises all over his body. He then went around the field area to check on the students. He found that almost all of the students had been hurt and a few were seriously injured. When he and the students looked for the school, they could see that it had been blown away, and all they could see where it had been was one of the desks, the bell, and a few timbers.

The Newman School destroyed by the tornado. (Photo courtesy of Barry Cleveland)

They also saw a house was still standing up northwest of where the school had been. This house, the Adam Lutz home, was just on the northwestern side of the intersection of County Roads 1600N and 750E. It had some damage, but it was still in good shape. Jasper told the students that they should go over there. So he and all of the students started walking over there. One of the boys carried one of the girls who was in such bad shape that she could not walk. After they got there, it was found how bad some had been hurt. Lorene and Charles found that their sister had a piece of wood that had blown under her scalp. She was in bad shape, but fortunately, she never died from it.

After a while, many of the parents came over to Adam Lutz's home to find their children who had been at the school. When John and Nannie Powers came over from their slightly damaged home that was next to Seven Mile Creek and County Road 1600N, they found that their daughter who had been at school was badly hurt. Fortunately, even though many students had been hurt, none died from their injuries. However, Jasper Mossberger received an infection from his injuries, and he died about three weeks later on April 9th.

Just after the tornado destroyed the Newman School, it hit Ed Young's home, an eighth of a mile northeast of the school. The tornado badly damaged his home, and after it went by, the remaining parts of the house caught on fire and burned up. Fortunately, no one was injured there, but Ed's daughter, who was at Newman School, was badly hurt with several broken bones.

As the tornado roared across County Road 800E, it caused damage for more than a mile along the road. About a half-mile north of County Road 1600N and on the west side of road, a barn on George Wagner's farm had its roof blown off. Since this was on the northern edge of the tornado as it passed by, there was nothing else damaged on George's farm. Along the road about a quarter-mile south of George's damaged barn, many fences next to the road had been blown down. A lot more fences were blown away farther south. On the southwestern side of the intersection of County Roads 800E and 1600N is where John Young's home was located. As the tornado hit his home, it was completely destroyed, and he and his wife, Celia, were hurt. Celia had her eyes injured and suffered a fractured arm. Also, John's niece, Lena, who lived with them, was at Newman School on that day, and she was seriously hurt. A piece of wood pierced her leg, and tetanus set in. She also got a bad scalp wound.

About a quarter-mile south of John Young's home and on the eastern side of County Road 800E was where Oral Warthen's home was located on the Speck farm. The tornado completely destroyed Oral's home, and his wife, Versie, was killed. Their four-year-old son, Harold Edward, was badly injured and died just a little bit later. Their baby, Wanda Mae, was able to stay alive.

About a half-mile south of Oral's home and on the western side of County Road 800E was William Puckett's home. It was near the southern edge of the tornado, but his home did get a part of its roof taken off. The top of his barn was shoved over, and it was left hanging there.

About a quarter-mile southeast of Oral Warthen's place and along County Road 1560N was where Emanuel Berry's home was located. As the tornado hit Emanuel's home, it was badly damaged. A large tree landed on the center part of the home's damage. Emanuel was not hurt, but his wife, Mary, sustained a bad head injury. On south along County Road 1560N, the woods had many of its trees torn down.

After the tornado completely destroyed the Newman School and John Young's home along County Road 1600N, it caused a lot more devastation along this road for the next two miles to the east. Less than a half-mile east of the John Young's place and on George Speck's farm was his son Fred Speck's home and barn that was on the northern side of the road. A little farther east on George's farm was his home, which was on the southern side of the road. His large barn was on the northern side of the road. As the tornado had reached White County, no one was in Fred's home because he and his wife, Edna, had gone over to George's home with their two young sons. Their daughters, Catherine and Evelyn, were at Newman School.

However, over at George's home, many people were there. In addition to Fred, Edna, and their sons, George's mother, Catherine "Kate" Speck, was there because she lived in his home then. Also, his daughter, Louise Robley, and her son, Roy, were at his home because they and Louise's husband, Ralph, were also living in his home at that time. Ralph, however, was not there at this time of day because he was doing some work somewhere else.

In this afternoon at George's home, it started getting dark outside, and it looked like it would soon be raining and getting stormy. Because of this, Fred Speck decided to go over to Newman School, pick up his daughters, and bring them back. As he started to go over to George's big barn to get his car, George told him that the storm looked too bad and he should not go. George also said that everyone should get into his cellar. He had most of them go outside with him, and over on the eastern side of the house, he showed them where to go down into his cellar. As they were going down into the cellar, George ran back into the house, got some valuable papers he needed, picked up his mother from her wheelchair, and rushed back toward the cellar. However, before he got out of the house, the tornado hit, and they did not get down in the cellar. Down in George's cellar, Louise's son, Roy, heard the tornado hitting the house and saw the top of the cellar go open as the floor above it was blown off to the east.

Roy Robley next to his home in April of 2005, and just after a windstorm had blown down some of his tree limbs. This home was where George Wagner lived in 1925, and George Speck brought his grandson, Roy Robley, and other family members up here to stay since this home was not damaged, and his had been destroyed. (Photo courtesy of Roy Robley, and taken by Bob Johns)

Roy, his mother, and the Fred Speck family got out of the cellar after the tornado was gone. They saw that George's home and his big barn on the northern side of the road were completely destroyed. Fred Speck's home and barn just northwest of them were completely destroyed. As they looked around where George's home had been, they found George and Kate and saw they had been very seriously injured. Kate had a broken leg, a cut over her right eye, and a gash in the back of her head. George had some type of two-by-four from the house blown into his chest, and it was hurting his lung. Because it had gotten cold after the tornado went by and George and Kate were in such bad shape, they looked around to see where they could go. The only home they could see that had not been damaged or destroyed was the George Wagner home, about three-quarters of a mile northwest of where they were. Fred said he would go up there and see if he could take George and Kate to that place because there was no known hospital they could take them to in this county.

While Fred was walking up there, some people came to George Speck's place to find those people who were there when the tornado occurred, and they wanted to help them. When Fred got back to his father's place, he saw that the people who had come to help them had a wagon. He asked them "can you use your wagon to take George, Kate, and the rest of us over to George Wagner's home?" The wagon owner said "I am really glad I can take all of you over there. Please get into my wagon right now." Once the people from George Speck's place got on the wagon, they were taken over there. When they got there, it was good to have George and Kate inside a home since it was cold outside, and they were not feeling good. Even though George Wagner's home was not damaged, they could see that his barn, which was south of his home, had its roof blown off. They also saw that the tornado had damaged Frank Ritsch's place, which was about a quarter-mile east of George Wagner's home, but it was not completely destroyed.

Fred and Edna Speck were concerned about their two daughters, Catherine and Evelyn, who had been in Newman School, and they thought it had likely been hit. After they had got to the George Wagner's home, they met someone there with a buggy who was planning to go to the Newman School area. They were pleased they could go over there in the buggy, and Roy and his mother, Louise, went with them, too. When they got there, they saw that the school had been destroyed. However, the Adam Lutz home next to it was still standing. They went over there and found that the students were there. Fred and Edna found that both of their daughters were there, but Evelyn had been badly injured. They were able to take their daughters with them back to George Wagner's home. The day after the tornado occurred, George Speck died from his lung problem injury. However, Kate and Evelyn did not die from their bad injuries.

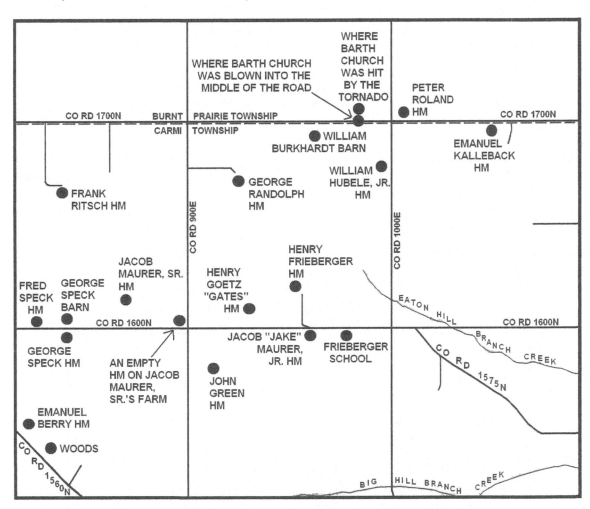

*Black circle points that show tornado damage locations in the middle north part of
Carmi Township and the southeast edge of Burnt Prairie Township.*

On east of the George Speck farm, along County Road 1600N, and just west of County Road 900E was Jacob Maurer Sr.'s farm. Jacob's home was about a quarter-mile northeast of George's home. As the tornado was coming, Jacob, his wife, Kate, his son, Reuben, and his daughters, Katie and Hellon, were at home. After completely destroying George's home and big barn, the tornado completely destroyed Jacob's home, barn, and outbuildings, and everyone there was injured. Jacob and Reuben were the most badly hurt. Jacob had several types of injuries, and one was his badly fractured leg. He was almost unable to walk after he was injured. Reuben had his ribs fractured, and he developed pneumonia. On Jacob's farm near the intersection of County Roads 1600N and 900E, the tornado also destroyed his empty house and the nearby barn and outbuildings.

On east of County Road 900E and close to County Road 1600N for a mile, there was a lot more destruction. Southeast of the intersection of County Roads 900E and 1600N was John Green's farm, and the tornado demolished his home and barn. Up on the northern side of County Road 1600N was Henry Gates's farm. Henry had changed his last name from "Goetz" to "Gates" some years before the tornado occurred. On the day of the tornado, Henry and his wife, Josephine, had been gone over to the town of Carmi. When they got home in the early afternoon, they had their two young sons, Carl and Ralph, with them. Carl went out in the yard, and he was playing. Ralph stayed in the house and decided to change his clothes. Henry and Josephine noticed it was getting dark outside and a storm was coming. Because it was going to get stormy, Henry went outside. He took his horses and cattle over to his barn and put them in there. As the tornado was about to get there, it got windy. As the wind broke some of the home's windows, Josephine stuck some pillows into the window openings. Then the tornado got there, and their home and barn were completely destroyed. Henry was inside the barn when it was demolished, but he was not hurt because a part of the barn sill fell down next to him. It stayed just above him and kept the other debris from crushing him. Josephine and Ralph were in their home when it was destroyed, and they were both hurt. Josephine was badly injured when something hit her head and almost tore off her scalp. The home's chimney crumbled down on Ralph and hurt his head, bruised his body, and caused him to become unconscious. Carl was out in the yard when the tornado hit, and a part of the destroyed home fell on top of him. His leg was all twisted up. When Henry got out of the barn area after the tornado was gone, he was able to find Josephine, Carl, and Ralph and realized they had been hurt. Henry was worried about his son, Glenard, and his daughter, Francis, who were at the Frieberger School when the tornado occurred. He would later find out that the school had been destroyed and they had been hurt. Glenard was only slightly hurt, but Francis had one of her arms broken and her hip injured.

Henry Gates's home destroyed by the tornado. (Photo courtesy of the Libraries in Carmi)

When Henry Gates was able to get his wife and all of his children together, he took them over to a relative's home in Carmi so they could be cared for. They were all able to stay alive. Several days later, farmer Joe Belcher called Henry and told him that he had found his cancelled check on his farm, twelve miles southeast of Vincennes, Indiana. The tornado had blown Henry's cancelled check fifty-eight miles away from where he lived. On the day after the tornado occurred, D.A. Bymm found Henry's postcard on the ground about a mile southwest of Bloomfield, Indiana, and Henry received it a few days later. The tornado had blown Henry's postcard ninety-five miles away from where he lived.

East of Henry Gates's farm and on the same side of the road was Henry Frieberger's farm. Similar to what the tornado did to the Gates's home and barn, the Frieberger's home and barn were also completely destroyed. South of the Frieberger farm and about a mile east-southeast of Jacob Maurer Sr.'s farm is where Jacob's oldest son, Jacob "Jake" Maurer Jr., lived on the southern side of County Road 1600N. Jake lived there with his wife, Susie, and their children. When the tornado hit his place, his home was blown off its foundation but not badly damaged. So no one in his home was injured.

The last place hit by the tornado along County Road 1600E was the Frieberger School, about two miles east of the Newman School. Similar to the Newman School, the Frieberger School was also completely destroyed. Most of the students there were injured, and nine-year-old Wilburn Felty was killed. The tornado blew away a paper that one of the students had written, and it landed ninety-five miles away in Bloomfield, Indiana. It was written in pencil and still clearly legible, so the person who found it could tell where it came from. The tornado also blew away a passbook that the teacher, Violetta Williams, had on her desk, and it landed about fifty-five miles away near Vincennes, Indiana. Violetta had gotten the passbook from a bank in Carmi, and when it was found near Vincennes, it was sent back to the bank. These two items from the school had landed close to where the two items that were blown away from Henry Gates's home landed.

Up north of Henry Gates's farm and Henry Frieberger's farm, the tornado was still causing damage along the northern edge of Carmi Township. About three-quarters of a mile north of Henry Gates's home was George Randolph's home. The tornado completely destroyed George's home. However, George was not hurt because he was visiting someone over in Indiana on that day. Northeast of George's place and on the northern edge of Carmi Township, the tornado destroyed two of the barns on William Burkhardt's farm. Just after the tornado caused this damage, it started causing damage in the southern edge of Burnt Prairie Township, which is on the northern side of County Road 1700N. It also continued to cause some damage on the northern edge of Carmi Township for about two miles to the east of where William's barns were destroyed.

About a quarter-mile southeast of William's damage, the tornado hit William Hubele Jr.'s home and barn, which were on his father-in-law's (Philip Fleck's) farm that was on the western edge of County Road 1000E. His home and barn were completely destroyed, and the home was blown away. William and his wife, Annie, were at home when the tornado hit, and they were both badly hurt. William had a scalp wound and a badly skinned leg, and his body was bruised. Annie had the end of one of her fingers torn off and got some bad bodily bruises. Their son, twenty-year-old Norman, was also hurt with fractured ribs and a bad scalp wound. Norman was either at his parents' home or some home he had already moved to before the tornado occurred, and it was destroyed. If he had already gotten into his new home, it would have been either on Phillip Fleck's farm or somewhere else nearby.

About a half-mile east-northeast of William Hubele's place and near the southern side of County Road 1700N was Emanuel Kalleback's home. The tornado badly damaged his home. About a half-mile east-southeast of Emanuel's place and on the western side of County Road 1100E was an empty house on Dr. John. T. Legier's farm that was badly damaged.

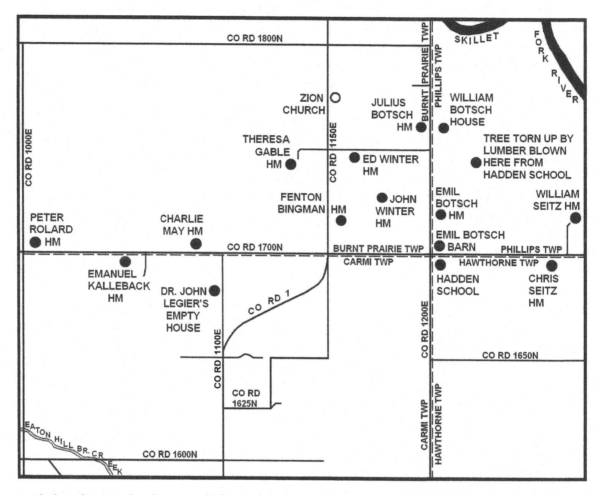

Black circle points that show tornado damage locations in the northeast part of Carmi Township, the southeast part of Burnt Prairie Township, the southwest part of Phillips Township, and the northwest edge of Hawthorne Township. One white circle point shows were a church was not hit by the tornado and was not damaged.

After the empty house was badly damaged on the Legier farm in northeastern Carmi Township, the tornado continued to cause a lot more damage in southeastern Burnt Prairie Township, and it is not known if there were any more homes or barns damaged before the tornado moved out of the northeastern edge of Carmi Township. As the tornado roared across Carmi Township, it stayed in a rural area and damaged or devastated more than twenty-eight homes and also destroyed Newman School and Frieberger School. Seven people were either instantly killed or badly injured and died later. Many more people were injured.

Burnt Prairie Township

In the southeastern part of the township from the Barth Church area to just southeast of the Zion Church

As the northern part of the mile-wide tornado roared into the southern edge of Burnt Prairie Township, it first hit the Barth Church, next to the Carmi-Burnt Prairie Township line and just on the northern side of County Road 1700N. When the church was hit, it was blown off its foundation to the south and landed in the middle of County Road 1700N. Although the church was badly damaged, it completely blocked the road. On farther east of the church and on the northeastern side of the intersection of County Roads 1700N and 1000E was Peter Roland's home. As the northern edge of the tornado hit his home, it blew off the roof but did not completely destroy it. Almost a mile farther east on the northern side of County Road 1700N, the tornado was getting farther up into Burnt Prairie Township. Charlie May's home was completely destroyed and blown away because a larger part of the tornado hit it. Charlie and his wife, Louise, saw one of their children get blown out of their windows as the home was being destroyed. Charles and some of their children who were not blown away were hurt. Later, they found that their child who had been blown out of the house and landed several yards away had also been hurt.

After the tornado hit the Barth Church, Peter Roland's home, and Charlie May's home on the southern edge of Burnt Prairie Township, it started getting up farther into the township as it was moving east-northeast. However, in just one more mile, it would move out of the eastern side of the township, which is along County Road 1200E. Even though the tornado was only going to be in a small part of the township, during this last mile, it did cause a lot of damage, and two people died from their injuries.

As it was about to reach County Road 1150E, it hit Theresa Gable's home and barn, and they were badly damaged. Theresa had debris fall on her in the house, and she was unable to get up because the rubble was on top of her. Her daughter, Edith, was able to get someone to come over and help her get the debris off her mother. Although Theresa was hurt when she was able to get up, she was able to stay alive.

Farther south and on the eastern side of County Road 1150E was Fenton Bingham's home. As the tornado hit his place, his home and outbuildings were destroyed. His wife, Nancy ("Susie"), was in the home when it was destroyed and was severely injured with a fractured jawbone and ankle. Her body was literally skinned all over. Susie's thirteen-year-old son, Herman, was over at the Hadden School in the northwestern edge of Hawthorne Township, about a half-mile east-southeast of their home. She would later find out that her son was killed over there.

East of Theresa Gable's place and less than a quarter-mile east of County Road 1150E was Ed Winter's home that was on his farm. About a quarter-mile southeast of Ed's home was where his father, John Winter, had his home on his farm. On the day of the tornado, Ed and John decided to go to a sale that was going on at John Weiss's place, which was on the western side of the Little Wabash River and northeast of the Skillet Fork River. Ed left his home with a buggy pulled with a team of mules. He stopped at John's home and picked him up. Then they went south to County Road 1700N and went west for about a mile and a half. When they got close to the Little Wabash River, they turned north into the Phillips Township area and stopped at Ben Kallenbach's place, just south of the Skillet Fork River. Because they could not drive across the Skillet Fork River, Ben got them on his boat and crossed over the river. Once they got on the northern side of the river, all three of them walked on up north for a half-mile to get to John Weiss's place for the sale. When the sale was over in the afternoon, they returned to Ben's place, and Ed and John got in the buggy and started home.

They noticed it was getting dark. It looked like a storm was coming from the west and it would be raining when it got there. As they were about to pass by Hadden School on County Road 1700N, Ed decided to stop there since he knew his daughter, Berniece, who had walked over to the school that morning, had not taken her overshoes with her. It would not be good for her to walk a long way home from the school when the ground got wet from the rain.

Since it was getting time for the school to close and she did not have any more stuff to do, he was able to put her in his buggy so he could take her home. He left his son, ten-year-old Edwin, there since he needed to stay until his lessons were done. He would not have any problem walking home if the ground were wet. As Ed left the school with John and Berniece also in the buggy, he had the mules take his buggy up to John's home. As they were going up there, they could see it was getting darker and stormier west of them. When Ed stopped at John's home and let his father get out of the buggy, John's wife, Lottie, came out of the house since she had been watching the storm that was coming. As she was looking west, she could see that the storm had a huge area where the dark clouds were rolling around on the ground. Lottie said, "Ed, you should not leave here. There is a storm coming that looks very dangerous" Ed said, "Berniece and I need to go on home since my wife and our other children are there now. I need to be there with them when the storm gets here." To get there quicker, he needed to take the buggy across the field between his father's home and his home rather than going back out to the road. John opened his gate so Ed could take his buggy across the field. He was able to get the mules to go as fast as they could. He started getting worried since he could see debris flying into the air over where the storm was west of them, and the storm sounded loud, like a train was coming. He told Berniece it was going to be bad.

At his home, his wife, Carrie, had the rest of her children with her there: eighteen-year-old Lena, fifteen-year-old Carl, thirteen-year-old Chester, six-year-old Herman, and baby Marie. A couple days before, Carrie had gotten some raspberry plants from a neighbor, and since the ground was dry, she was waiting for rain before she would set up the plants. As she first noticed there would be a storm coming on this day and it was likely to rain, she decided to go out to the lower part of the garden and set up the plants. She took her young son, Herman, with her. After she had set several of the plants down, she noticed the storm looked dangerous. She started hearing a noise like a train that was over where the storm was west of her. She looked over there and saw many black clouds that looked like smoke, and they were moving around on the ground and up above. This really worried her, and she told Herman that they had to return to the house.

At the same time, both Carrie and her husband, Ed, were getting worried about the storm that was getting close to them. Carrie picked up Herman in the garden and started running toward their home. When she got there, they went in the backdoor and got into the kitchen. As Ed and Berniece were coming across the field in their buggy as fast as they could and were getting close to their place, the wind got so strong that the buggy was being shifted some. At his home, Carl saw them coming, and he ran outside to help them. Ed stopped the buggy next to his barn so he could move the mules from the buggy into the barn. Carl had gotten there, and he was going to help him. However, Ed first picked up Berniece and put her in the small walkway part of the barn that would be safer for her. He told her that she should stay inside this part of the barn since she would likely be blown away if she walked on toward her home. He shut the door where she was so she would stay in there. He went out to the buggy with Carl to take the mules over to the other part of the barn. It started raining while they were doing this, and just after Ed and Carl got the mules inside the other side of the barn where many horses were, the tornado hit Ed's place.

As the tornado hit Ed's barn and destroyed it, Berniece was standing next to the barn door in the walkway, and she saw the barn trying to rise up off the ground three times. The third time, it was destroyed, and part of it fell back down on her. She was knocked down beside the concrete foundation. A horse that was blown down next to her had one of its legs on top of her. Because the horse appeared to be knocked out, it did not move its leg off of her. Berniece's legs had been bruised, but they were not broken. Ed and Carl were blown out of the barn as it was destroyed and landed in the horse lot. Ed had debris blown on him, but he was not hurt. Carl was also not hurt.

As the tornado was hitting their home, Carrie was there with four of her children. Just as she got into a bedroom and had picked Marie off the cradle, a wall clock was blown off. It hit Carrie on her shoulder and then knocked her down on the floor. She had the other three children with her nearby, and as the clock fell down on her, all also saw the home windows and frames being blown out. They could also feel the home being moved off its foundation and being twisted around. A part of its roof was torn off. This really scared them. But fortunately, the home was not destroyed, and they were not hurt much. Just near the home, the tornado damaged the car shed. Their Overland car was blown out of there. It passed over the backyard and landed in the chicken yard.

Once the tornado was gone from Ed's place, it was raining hard, and some hail was falling. Ed and Carl went over to where their damaged home had been blown, and they were glad to get inside since it was raining hard and hailing. Carrie and the others in the home had not been hurt. Because Ed did not see Berniece there, he asked Carrie if she knew where she was. Carrie did not know that Ed had brought Berniece from the school and put her in the barn before it was destroyed. So when Ed told Carrie what he had done, they both got worried about Berniece, and they went over to where the barn had been to see if they could find her. It was still raining but not hailing. They saw a lot of the lumber, timber, horses, and some mules on the ground where the barn had been, and they did not see her. Some yelled to find where she was, and when she heard then yelling, she yelled back to them. They then knew where she was on the ground. They went over to where they heard her, moved away the horse, and then dug timber and lumber off of her so they could get her up. Her legs were bruised, but she was not hurt much. Since the rain and hail had quit, it was easier for her to walk back to the home with her mother.

Ed and Carl then started pulling lumber and timber off the mules and horses. When Ed found one of the mules that had brought him back home in the buggy, he had to pull a heavy piece of timber off of him. His collar was broken in two places. While Ed and Carl were still working on the horses and mules, they saw a neighbor, Edyth Gable, who had walked over from her place, which was west of them. She told them that she needed help getting her mother up out of debris where their home was badly damaged.

Because this let Ed know that damage occurred well away from his place, he looked down southeast where his parents' farm was, and he was really worried when he saw that their home, barn, and all of their other outbuildings had been destroyed and flattened with nothing standing up there at all. He and Carl decided to run down there and see if they could find Ed's parents. Even though they had to leave, Edyth got someone else to come to her place and help her get her mother out of the debris.

When Ed and Carl started walking across the field to get to John and Lottie's place, they saw there had been a lot of rain since some of the ditches had been flooded. Then when they got to John and Lottie's place and started looking around to find them, they first found Lottie. She was badly hurt, and her shoulder was crushed. Although she was in bad shape, she was able to talk to them.

She said she had not been able to find her husband. So Ed and Carl said they would try to find him. After looking around for a while, they found him on the ground, and he was so badly hurt that he was unconscious. Ed decided he should take his parents over to his home. After he and Carl got them over there, Ed wanted Carl to go get a doctor as quick as he could since John and Lottie were in such bad shape. Ed was able to have his parents checked on fairly soon, but John died several days later. Lottie died several days after John did.

Somewhere in the southeastern part of Burnt Prairie Township near John Winter's place or Fenton Bingman's place is where Tom Brooks's place was located. The tornado destroyed Tom's house and barn.

The last place hit in Burnt Prairie Township was Julius Botsch's home. It was east-northeast of Ed Winter's place and on the western side of County Road 1200E. Julius's home and outbuildings were destroyed. His wife, Lora, was at home when it was destroyed. When she was found, she was on a door that had been blown down, and it had some wood, splinters, and nails in it. When someone found her, he lifted the door up with her on it and took her up to a home that had not been damaged farther north of County Road 1200E.

Even though the tornado only partially came into Burnt Prairie Township during the last two miles while it was moving along the Burnt Prairie-Carmi Township line, it damaged or devastated at least seven homes and the Barth Church. Two people were badly injured and died later. Also, several people were injured.

Hawthorne Township

In the northwestern edge of this township and at Hadden School and just east of there.

The tornado mostly passed by to the north of Hawthorne Township, but it did hit two places on the northern edge of the township line near the northwestern edge of the township. Hadden School was right next to the northwestern edge of Hawthorne Township, and the students lived in homes that were in four different townships within a mile of the school: Carmi, Burnt Prairie, Phillips, and Hawthorne. As the tornado hit the Hadden School, it was completely destroyed. The big iron bell on the school was blown about a quarter mile away. Also, a two-by-four stick of lumber from the school was blown about a half-mile north-northeast into Phillips Township. It was embedded in a tree, and the tree was cut up. Quite a few people were in the school. Student Herman Bingman, the son of Fenton and "Susie" Bingman who lived in Burnt Prairie Township, was killed. Many of the other students were injured, but no one else was killed. Student Edwin Winter, the son of Ed and Carrie Winter who lived in Burnt Prairie Township, and the schoolteacher, Ernest Lamp, were blown into a field about a quarter-mile away from where the school had been. But fortunately, they were not hurt very much.

The Hadden School destroyed by the tornado. (Photo courtesy of the Libraries in Carmi)

About a half-mile east of where the school was and on the southern side of County Road 1700N was where the tornado hit Chris Seitz's home. His home and his barn were blown away. He was at home when it happened, and he was badly injured with a broken leg. He also had many bruises on his body.

Even though the tornado did not get into Hawthorne Township very much, quite a few people were injured, and one person was killed just on the northwestern edge of the township.

Phillips Township

From just north of Nadden School in the southwestern edge of the township to passing by just south of Crossville and to near the Wabash River north of Poplar Ridge Church

As the tornado roared into southwest Phillips Township, it first hit Emil Botsch's barn, which was next to Nadden School but on the northern side of County Road 1700N. Emil's barn was destroyed. As the tornado hit Emil's home north of his barn, it was badly damaged but not destroyed. And the people there were only slightly injured. About a half-mile farther north of Emil's place was the location of a house that his father, William Botsch, owned. As the tornado was about to hit William's house, it had already hit his two son's homes, Emil's home to the south and Julius's home close by on the western side of County Road 1200E in Burnt Prairie Township. When the tornado crossed the road and hit William's house in Phillips Township, it was picked up and then slammed down into its basement. No one was injured in William's house when it was hit.

After the tornado had hit Emil and William Botsch's places, as it was roaring into the southwestern edge of Phillips Township, it then hit William Seitz's home almost three-quarters of a mile east of Emil's home. As the tornado was approaching, William's wife, Alvina, and their two-year old daughter, Marjorie, were at home. Alvina heard the storm coming, and it seemed to be getting dark outside. So she closed all of the windows in their house. Then she and Marjorie ran over to their nearby barn for shelter. Just after they got there, the tornado hit their place, and their home was completely destroyed. The barn was not destroyed, and they were not hurt. William was working in Grayville when the tornado came by, so he was north of where the tornado was causing damage. However, William and Alvina's daughters, Frances and Berneda, were about three-quarters of a mile away from home at Haddon School in Hawthorne Township. That was not a good place for them to be when the tornado came by since the school was destroyed.

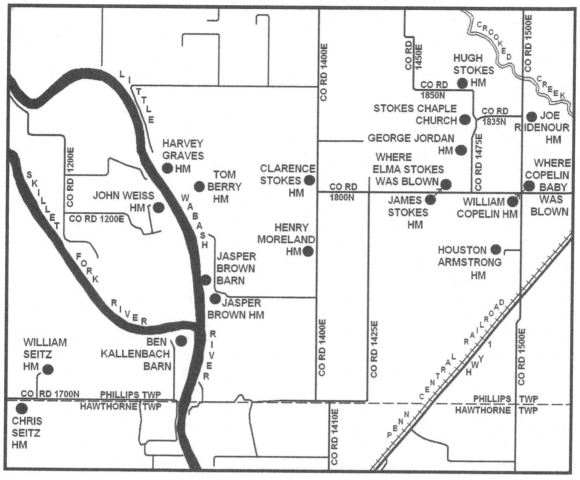

*Black circle points that show tornado damage locations in the northwest edge of Hawthorne Township and the
southwest part of Phillips Township. In two places on this map, a line from one black circle point to another black
circle point shows where people got blown away from, and where they landed.*

As the mile-wide tornado roared on across Phillips Township, it caused a lot of devastation. As
it crossed over the Little Wabash River area, it caused damage at five places next to the river. The
two places on the western side of the river were Ben Kallenbach's place close to where the Skillet
Fork River meets with the Little Wabash River and John Weiss's place, about three-quarters of a mile
farther north. On the day of the tornado, John was having a sale at his place. Ben came over to his
place for the sale with Ed and John Winter, and some others were there. After the sale was over and
all the people had left, the tornado hit John's place. His home was very badly damaged, and his barn
was destroyed. After Ben had left the sale and got to his place, he saw the tornado coming. Since his
place was near the southern edge of the tornado as it was going by, his home was not damaged. But
his barn was badly hurt.

As the tornado got on the eastern side of the river, it hit Harvey Graves's place, Tom Berry's
home that was on William Moser's place, and Jasper Brown's place. Harvey Grave's home is north of
John Weiss's home and on the other side of the river. After the tornado damaged John's place, it hit
Harvey's home and blew it away. Harvey was at home when this happened, and he was hurt. He had
to be treated for his bad bodily bruises. Southeast of Harvey's home is where Tom Berry's home was
on William Moser's place. Tom's home was destroyed, and one of his family members was severely

121

injured. Along the river about a half-mile south of Tom's home was where Jasper Brown's home and barn were. As the tornado hit his place, it blew away his barn and damaged his home. Fortunately, no one was badly hurt there.

As the tornado roared away from the river area and was crossing County Road 1400E, it hit Henry Moreland's home on the George Brown farm and Clarence Stokes's place. Henry's home was blown away, and he and his wife were badly injured. After the tornado was gone, they were taken to a hospital. They were treated, and they were in good enough shape to leave the hospital four days after they were injured. About a quarter-mile north of Henry's home along County Road 1400E was where Clarence Stokes's place was. As the tornado hit Clarence's place, his home and barn were destroyed. Clarence's wife, Stella, was not hurt, but Clarence and their eight-year-old son, Aquila, were both injured. Clarence's right leg was badly fractured, and he got a scalp wound and some other bodily bruises. Aquila's leg was broken in two places, and he had numerous scalp wounds.

A half-mile east of Clarence's place and on the southern side of County Road 1800N was James Stokes's place. As the tornado was approaching, James noticed a threatening dark cloud coming toward his home. So he decided to go down into his cellar, which was outside his backdoor and just west of the house. He begged his wife, Elma, to go down there with him. She did go outside with him to where the cellar was located. But when she saw the cellar, she got scared and feared they could not get out after the storm had gone by. As James was going down into the cellar, Elma ran back into the house. Just after she got there, the tornado hit their place. From the cellar, James could see his house get swept away. Elma was also blown away, and she landed about fifty yards from where the home had been. As soon as the tornado was gone, James came up out of the cellar as fast as he could to find his wife. When he got up above the cellar and looked around, he saw that his barn had also been blown away and Elma was not where his home had been. After he looked around on his place and nearby, he found Elma over on the north side of the road. He saw she was on the ground and she looked black and blue. As he picked her up, she only gasped once and then died.

About a quarter-mile north-northeast of James's place was where George and Sallie Jordan's large home was located on the western side of County Road 1475E. It was just south of the Stokes Chapel Church. George had done a lot of unusual things within his home, like set up a barbershop in one of his rooms. Also, he had made extra rooms in his house so that, when his sons and daughters got married, their families could live there. In March 1925, his son, Enos, and his wife, Fay, lived there. His son, Revis, and his wife lived there as well. However, in that same month, George was selling his farm to William W. Stokes.

On the day of the tornado, Fay and Revis's wife were in George's home. Also, since William had just bought George's place, he came over that day in his car with some carpenters to do some work on the barn. While William was working there, he noticed a big cloud coming from the west, and to him, it looked like big, black smoke right on the ground. Then he realized it was a tornado, and he told everyone they needed to get down into the cellar that was near there. As they were going down there, some of the people from George's home were also going down there. Just after they all got into the cellar, the tornado had arrived, and the top of the cellar was blown off. After the tornado was gone and they got out of the cellar, William saw that his car had been torn up. Also, he and the others saw that the home and barn had been destroyed. Since Revis's wife and Fay were still in the home when the tornado hit, they were both injured. Revis's wife was seriously injured as a stove from a neighbor's house, likely James Stokes's home, blew through the roof and fell on her as the house was being destroyed. One of the bones in her neck was broken.

As the tornado was destroying George Jordan's home and barn, it was also hitting the Stokes Chapel Church just north of there on the western side of County Road 1475E. The church was totally destroyed and leveled while most of church debris was blown off to the west of where the church had been. The cemetery next to the church had many of its monuments blown down. Up north of the church area is where Hugh Stokes's place was just west of County Road 1475E and on the northern side of County Road 1850N. Hugh and several of his sisters were not home when the tornado was approaching. Hugh's nephew, Martin, and a few others were there, and they were in the kitchen as the tornado was approaching. When the tornado hit Hugh's place, his barn was completely destroyed, and his two-story home was almost completely demolished. The only part of his home that was not completely destroyed was the kitchen. It was damaged a bit but still standing. Because those at home when the tornado arrived were in the kitchen, they were not injured.

The Stokes Chapel Church before it was hit by the tornado. (Photo courtesy of Linda Kuykendall)

The Stokes Chapel Church after it was destroyed by the tornado. (Photo courtesy of Linda Kuykendall)

After the tornado caused destruction at several places along and near County Road 1475E, it roared on to the east and caused more damage and destruction along and near County Road 1500E. About a quarter-mile east of the Stokes Chapel Church and on the eastern side of County Road 1500E, the tornado hit Joe Ridenour's home and barn that were on Boss Graves's farm. Joe's home was blown away, and his barn was demolished. Almost a half-mile south of Joe's place and on the southwestern side of the intersection of County Roads 1500E and 1800N was William Copelin's place, and about a quarter-mile on south of William's place and on the western side of County Road 1500E was Houston Armstrong's place.

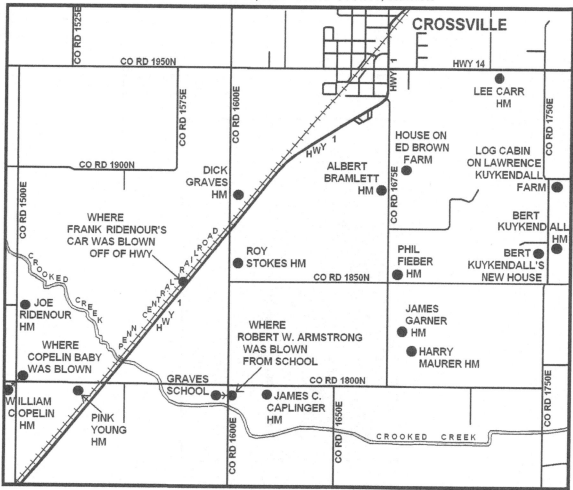

Black circle points that show tornado damage locations in the southwest and middle south part of Phillips Township near the town Crossville. In two places on this map, a line from one black circle point to another black circle point shows where people got blown away from, and where they landed.

In the early morning, nine-year-old Robert W. Armstrong, Houston's son, was working on his family's garden before he was going to school. He noticed it was cloudy that morning but not very windy. Just after eight in the morning, he and his brother, Smith, started walking to Graves School, a mile and a quarter east-northeast of where they lived. They needed to be there by nine. As they walked north along County Road 1500E, they passed by William Copelin's home just as they were about to turn east on County Road 1800N. As they were walking east on that road, they passed by Pink Young's home and then crossed over the Penn Central Railroad and Highway 1. On east of there, they passed over the Crooked Creek and made it to the school just before nine. As they were at school, Robert noticed it was cloudy during the rest of the morning and not very windy. However, during the afternoon, the tornado was coming, and the weather got a lot worse. Student Lavern Stokes, Roy Stokes's son, looked out of the school's west window and saw a large, black cloud coming, and it really worried him. He ran over to the teacher, Scigal Martin, and told him what he saw. The teacher went to the window, and he saw how bad it looked outside. He quickly told his sixteen students to go out of the school and lay down in the ditch next to the coal house, just a few feet northeast of the school and close to County Road 1600E.

When everyone started to get out of the school, the tornado was getting close. And about one-and-a-quarter mile west-southwest of the school, it was hitting the Houston Armstrong farm where Robert and his brother had walked from over to the school. At that place, the barn was mostly blown away, and the home was damaged. The tornado blew the chimney off their house and cut holes into the roof. Fortunately, none of Robert's family members was hurt there.

Robert W. Armstrong next to his home in April of 2005. He was blown out of Graves School when it was hit by the 1925 tornado. (Photo courtesy of Robert W. Armstrong, and taken by Bob Johns)

William Copelin had been south of his home and was working near Houston's farm as the tornado was coming. When he saw it, he started going back home as fast as he could since his wife, Alma, their little baby, Elizabeth, and their young son, Warren, were up there. However, as it was about to hit him before he got up there, he laid down in a ditch next to the road and held on to a fence post as the tornado got there. Some of his clothing was blown away, but fortunately, he was not hurt. As the tornado was hitting his home, Alma was lying on her bed and holding her baby. Her young son was somewhere else in the home. As their home and outbuildings were being blown away to the northeast, Elizabeth was pulled off of Alma's arms and blown away to the northeast. She landed on a mattress on the other side of the road intersection. Fortunately, she was not badly injured when she landed and was only hurt a little bit when some hail fell on her after she landed. Alma and Warren were not blown very far away when the house was destroyed. Warren was not hurt much, but Alma was seriously injured when some debris hit her. She had a gash on her head.

As the tornado roared on toward the school along County Road 1800N, it next hit Pink and Effie Young's place and badly damaged their home and barn. A collie dog that Pink and Effie had never seen before was blown through a window of their home. When they later looked at the dog, they found it was not badly hurt.

After causing damage on Pink and Effie's place, the tornado roared on along County Road 1800N and crossed the Penn Central Railroad, Highway 1, and the Crooked Creek. Then it was about to hit

Graves School. Just before the tornado got there, most of the students had opened one of the school's two north doors and walked along the hallway. Then they got out of the hallway and laid down in the ditch on the eastern edge of the coal house. Scigal, Robert W. Armstrong, and one of the other students had tried to open the school's other north door so they could go through the hallway and go outside to the ditch near the coal house. But they could not get that door open before the tornado hit the school. As it slammed into the school, it was torn up. Scigal, Robert, and the other student were blown away from where they were standing in the school. Robert was blown east of the school, and he landed in a ditch on the eastern side of County Road 1600E. When he was able to see where he was, he noticed several big trees had been blown down right next to him. Fortunately, he found that he had not been hurt. As he was walking back to where the school had been, he noticed the coal house was still standing and the students who had been lying down in a ditch next to the coal house had also not been hurt. However, when he found Scigal, who had been blown out of the school, he noticed he had been hurt with a scratch on his forehead. He appeared to be the only person at the school who had been injured. As Robert continued to look around the school area, he noticed Scigal's car had been blown away and the school had been completely flattened. The wall that had been on the southern side of the school had been blown down onto many of the students' seats in the school, and it had completely destroyed them. He was really pleased that Scigal told him and the others to leave their seats and go outside. Even though he was not able to get outside, it would have been very bad if he had stayed in his seat because the wall would have fallen down on him.

*A view of the ditch on the east side of County Road 1600E in April of 2005, where Robert W. Armstrong
had landed after he was blown away from Graves School by the tornado in 1925.
(Photo courtesy of Robert W. Armstrong, and taken by Bob Johns)*

A view of the storm cellar in April of 2005 that was built next to the new rebuilt Graves School after the 1925 tornado occurred. The rebuild Graves School was not there when this picture was taken. The reason why rural schools were not needed to be just two-miles apart after 1925 was because School Buses became more common to use, and students did not have to walk to school. (Photo courtesy of Robert W. Armstrong, and taken by Bob Johns)

After the tornado destroyed Graves School, it hit James C. Caplinger's farm, just east of the school and on the southern side of County Road 1800N. James's home and outbuildings were damaged but not destroyed. Because Graves School and James's farm were near the southern edge of the mile-wide tornado as it was roaring by, there was a lot more damage between County Road 1800N and Crossville. Frank Ridenour was driving along Highway 1 from Carmi to Crossville when the tornado was coming. When he saw the bad storm coming, he decided to drive as fast as he could and get to Crossville before it got to the highway. However, after he had driven past County Road 1800N and crossed over Crooked Creek, he realized the tornado was coming so fast that it was going to hit his car before he got up to Crossville. So he stopped his car on the edge of the highway, got out, and laid down in a ditch next to the road. The tornado picked up his car, and it was blown north and destroyed when it was knocked down against the railroad track. Fortunately, Frank was not hurt much since he was lying in the ditch when the tornado roared by.

After the tornado destroyed Frank's car along Highway 1, it roared on east-northeast and crossed County Road 1600E. It caused destruction on Roy Stokes's farm and Dick Graves's farm. As it hit Roy's place, it almost destroyed his home and completely destroyed his barn. Roy and his wife, Cora, and some of their children were at home when it was hit, and they were all hurt and suffered from bad bodily bruises. Their son, Lavern, was at Graves School, and he was not hurt since he got out of the school and laid down in a ditch.

Almost a half-mile north of Roy's place was where Dick Graves's home and barn were located. As the northern edge of the mile-wide tornado roared through his farm, his home and barn were damaged but not almost and completely destroyed like Roy's home and barn were.

Roy Stokes's home almost destroyed by the tornado. (Photo courtesy of the Libraries in Carmi)

As the mile-wide tornado roared on east-northeast across County Road 1675E and was just south of Crossville, it hit four occupied homes, three unoccupied houses, and a lot of barns and outbuildings. They were all damaged or destroyed. About a mile-and-a-quarter south of Crossville and on the eastern side of County Road 1675E was where James Garner's farm was hit. His home and barn on the northern side of his farm were damaged. On his farm was a tenant house that was south of his home, and Harry and Barbara Maurer lived there. They were both in their house as the tornado was coming, and their five-year-old son, Herschel, was also there. As the tornado hit their house, it was very badly torn up. Part of it was blown away into the field, and the rest of it fell down in the house area as debris. The crushed heating stove in the house area started a fire in the debris. Harry had not been badly hurt by the debris falling on him as the tornado was going by, but when he saw that his house had been destroyed and the debris had caught on fire, he was worried about what might have happened to his wife and son. He quickly got up and started looking for them. He found Herschel with some debris on him, and some of the fire was burning him. Harry quickly pulled the debris off him and picked him up. And while he was doing this, he was able to keep from getting burned himself. He took his son into a safe place out of the fire area, and when he set him down, he noticed that Herschel's hand had been burned. This really worried him. Harry quickly ran back into the house debris area and tried to find Barbara. As he was doing this, the fire was getting very dangerous since it was increasing through the area. As he kept searching for his wife, he started getting burned a lot, and if he kept staying in the fire area, he was likely to be killed. He left the area with his son and hoped to find some fireman who could stop the fire. However, he was not able to find someone to do that.

The next morning, he and others came over to see if they could find Barbara. The fire was over, so they were able to find where she was. She had been trapped down under the heating stove that had fallen on her body. She had been very badly burned and died.

Up north of James Garner's farm and just northeast of the intersection of County Road's 1675E and 1850N was Phillip "Phil" Fieber's farm. When the tornado hit their farm, Phil and his wife, Susan, were up at a funeral in Grayville. When they came back in their buggy, they saw their home, barn, trees, and tenant house about one hundred yards away from their home were all blown away. The only thing they saw that was still there was their well that was bricked up. When they looked down there, they saw many chickens were still alive, but they did not have any feathers on them. After they left the well area, they saw their old mule walking near them, and they noticed it was badly hurt because quite a few pieces of wood had been blown through its body. They were able to get some of the wood off its body, and it survived. After they had looked around, they realized the clothes they already had on were the only items they now had from their home.

About a half-mile north of where Phillip Fieber's home had been and on the western side of County Road 1675E was Albert Bramlett's home on his farm. His home was considered to be the most beautiful rural home in White County. Also on this farm was a tenant house, but it was unoccupied. As the tornado hit his farm, the tenant house was blown away. However, when his large home that he and his wife, Bessie, lived in was hit, it was not destroyed. Part of its roof was blown off, and some of the windows were blown out, but Albert and Bessie were not hurt. They were surprised when they found that the tornado had blown a fresh egg onto their front porch as it was going by.

Albert Bramlett's really nice home that was damaged by the tornado. (Photo courtesy of Linda Kuykendall)

Over northeast of Albert's home and on the eastern side of County Road 1675E was an unoccupied tenant house on Ed Brown's farm. As the tornado came by, it blew the roof off his tenant house. This house was the farthest one north along County Road 1675E that the tornado damaged, and it was just a quarter-mile south of Crossville. As the tornado was moving close by Crossville, it also hit Lee Carr's home, about a quarter-mile east of Crossville and on the southern side of Highway 14. Lee's home was damaged but not destroyed.

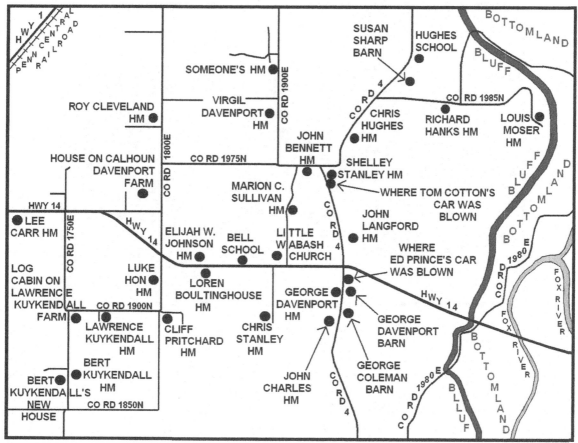

Black circle points that show tornado damage locations in the middle and east part of Phillips Township.

As the tornado was roaring across County Road 1750E, it hit the farms of Lawrence Kuykendall and Bert Kuykendall, who were brothers. Lawrence's farm was on the eastern side of the road and on the southern side of County Road 1900N. As the tornado was getting to his farm, it first hit his unoccupied tenant place where there was a log cabin house, a chicken house, and a barn. They were all blown away, and nothing was left there. Farther east on his farm was another barn and a home where he, his wife, Agnes, and their son, Eugene, lived. They were in their home when it and their barn were hit. Their home and barn were completely destroyed. Lawrence was seriously hurt. Agnes and Eugene were also injured, but not as bad as Lawrence was. However, Agnes had one of her legs hurt, and because it was hurting her, she did not feel that she could walk anywhere. Even though Lawrence was more badly hurt, he told her that he would carry her when they decided where to go from this unlivable place.

Lawrence Kuykendall's home destroyed by the tornado. (Photo courtesy of Linda Kuykendall)

Down south of Lawrence's farm was where his brother, Bert Kuykendall, had his farm that was on both sides of County Road 1750E. The home where Bert and most of his family members lived was on the eastern side of the road in a two-story house with six bedrooms, a bathroom, a generator, and a power plant. Bert also had another new house that he had built over on the western side of the road, and some of his older children who were married lived there. On the day of the tornado, Bert and his older sons, Frank and Lloyd, were building a fence over near his new house. While they were doing this, they saw the tornado roaring toward them. So they ran over into his new house before the tornado hit. When the tornado hit his new house, the windows were blown out, and the roof was blown off. Because it was not destroyed, they were not hurt. Near his new home, he found that a barn and two outbuildings had been blown away.

As the tornado was roaring toward Bert's home on the eastern side of the road, his wife, Laura, and their twenty-eight-year-old daughter, Flora, were there. When the tornado hit his home, it was twisted around and damaged. But it was not destroyed, and Laura and Flora were not hurt. When Bert got back home after the tornado was gone, he was pleased to find that his home was not destroyed and his wife and daughter were not hurt. As he looked around near his home, he found that his barn and outbuildings had been destroyed. He also found that several of his hogs and chickens had been killed. When he found his favorite buggy horse, Matz, he noticed something was blown through its neck and it was badly hurt. Sometime later, his horse died from this neck injury.

Later in the day, Bert's seriously hurt brother, Lawrence, brought his wife and son down to Bert's home that was still standing because they needed someplace they could stay. Lawrence had to carry his wife, Agnes, down there because her leg injury kept her from being able to walk. Bert was pleased that they got to his home and could stay there.

As the mile-wide tornado roared on across County Road 1800E farther east-northeast, several places along that road were known to be hit. East of Lawrence Kuykendall's farm and on the eastern side of the road was Cliff Pritchard's home and barn. As the tornado was coming toward his place, his wife, Sarah, was in their house with her baby, Lewis, who was less than a year old. And Cliff was out in his car with his farmhand. Sarah saw the tornado coming, so she took her baby into her bedroom and placed him on the bed. She bundled him in some quilts and gave him a bottle. As the tornado hit their place, their home and barn were blown away, and Sarah and her baby were also blown out of where the house had been. Sarah was not blown very far from where the house had been, but she was hurt. Her baby had been blown farther away, and she could not see him from where she was. When the tornado hit Cliff's car, it was damaged. He and the farmhand were blown out of it. Fortunately, they were not hurt.

When the tornado was gone, Cliff ran over to where his house had been, and he found Sarah and saw that she had been hurt. Because the baby was not near where she was, Cliff started going around his farm area to find the baby. He was also looking for his older son, Victor, who would have been walking home from Bell School about this time. He saw Victor running toward him. And when he got there, Cliff found the tornado had hit him up at Luke Hon's place, but he was not hurt much. After finding Victor, Cliff found the baby in a field. He had Victor go get Sarah and have her come over where the baby was found. When Sarah got there, she noticed her baby was still wrapped in quilts and still had the bottle. Fortunately, he was not hurt. Now that they were all together and their home had been destroyed, they went over to the home of Sarah's mother and were able to stay there.

Less than a quarter-mile north of Cliff's home and on the western side of County Road 1800N was where Luke Hon's home was. On the day of the tornado, Luke and his wife, Emma, were at home. When it was getting stormy in the afternoon, their sons, Arnold and Jim, and all of the other students were dismissed from Bell School, about a half-mile east-northeast of Luke's home and on the northern side of Highway 14. Arnold and Jim walked west on Highway 14, and when they got to County Road 1800E, they turned south and walked about an eighth-of-a-mile to get home. Several other students had been walking along with them because they had to pass by Luke Hon's home as they were going on farther to get to their homes. As Arnold and Jim were reaching their home and the other students walking with them were about to walk on by Luke Hon's home, they could all see that a dangerous storm was coming. Arnold and Jim were really glad they were getting home. Their father, Luke Hon, had also seen the bad storm coming. When he saw the other students stopping by his place when his sons were coming in, he ran outside and asked the other students to come into his home since the bad storm was about to hit them. Bert and Laura Kuykendall's three schoolchildren, Wilma, Oscar ("Buck"), and Charles ("Bud"), decided to go into Luke's home since he asked them to, and they were about three-quarters of a mile away from their home that was farther southeast. Cliff and Sarah Pritchard's son, Victor, also decided to go into Luke's home since he asked him to, and Victor was about a quarter-mile away from his home, which was farther south. In Luke's house, he had his sons and the other students come into his living room, and he told them sit down on the floor. When they got down on the floor, "Bud" noticed the dishes in the kitchen nearby were rattling, hail was pounding on the roof, and the wind was howling. Then he noticed that the house windows were all breaking, and as he looked up above, he saw plaster was falling down as the roof was being blown away. That was the last thing "Bud" was able to see as the tornado was destroying Luke's home and barn and swept them away. After the tornado was gone, Luke had been hurt but not badly. So he started looking around and saw that the house was gone and the floor had been blown behind the house. He fell down in his orchard. As he checked on his wife, he found she had a hurt leg. As he checked on the students, he found that his son, Arnold, had a lot of plaster rubble that had fallen on top of him. Luke was able to dig Arnold up out of the debris, and he found that he had been hurt. Some of the other students had also been hurt. But fortunately, Luke found that no one at his place had been seriously injured. Since the tornado was gone, Cliff Pritchard's son, Victor, and Bert Kuykendall's children decided to run on to their homes and find out what happened there.

133

About a half-mile north of Luke Hon's home and on the western side of County Road 1800E was an old, unoccupied house on Calhoun Davenport's farm. When the tornado hit, it was badly damaged. About a mile north of where Cliff Pritchard's home and Luke Hon's home were completely destroyed is where Roy Cleveland's home was located on the western side of County Road 1800E. This was the only home along this road that Cliff and Luke could see that was still standing. Roy's home was near the northern edge of the tornado path, and it was only slightly damaged with some of its windows broken out.

As the tornado moved on east of County Road 1800E, it was roaring along Highway 14 where the Bell School was located and where the students had walked along when they were going home from school. There was almost complete destruction along this part of the highway, so it was good that all of the students were not still in school or walking along the highway when the tornado roared through there.

Along the highway between County Road 1800E and the County Road 4, the tornado hit Elijah Johnson's home, Loren Boultinghouse's place, Bell School, and the Little Wabash Church. As the tornado hit Loren's place on the southern side of the road, his home was the only building along this area that was not completely destroyed. His home was badly damaged, and his barn was destroyed and blown away. On the northern side of the road near Loren's place was where Elijah Johnson's home was located. Elijah and his wife, Laura, were at home when the tornado hit their place. It destroyed their home and blew it away. Laura had gotten near her heavy refrigerator. She was not blown away, and she was not hurt. Elijah did get blown away from where he was standing, and he fell down by the side of a concrete pillar. He was seriously hurt and suffered a bad gash on his head and a broken leg.

About a quarter-mile east of Elijah's home was Bell School, and it was also on the northern side of Highway 14. On the day of the tornado, teacher Percy Rawlinson was teaching the students. It started getting stormy in the afternoon. George Davenport, who lived about a half-mile east of the school, noticed a dangerous-looking cloud was showing up in the storm area somewhere west of him. He got into his Model-T and drove over to Bell School to pick up his two grandsons, John and Hal Davenport, who lived with him. He got there at about three o'clock, and he told the teacher that a dangerous black cloud was coming toward this area. Since it might be a tornado, he wanted to take his grandsons home if it were okay. Percy told him that it was okay to take them home, and George put them in his car and started going home. Just after they left, Percy told the other students that they should go home as well since the storm looked bad. So the school was dismissed, and all of them, including the schoolchildren of Luke Hon, Cliff Pritchard, and Bert Kuykendall, started walking home. Percy stayed at the school, and the tornado hit almost an hour after George had let him know that it was coming. The school was completely blown away, and afterwards, you could not tell there had been a building on the site. Percy was hurt when she was hit, and she had a head injury.

Less than a quarter-mile east of the school and on the northern side of Highway 14 was the Little Wabash Baptist Church. When the church was hit, it was completely destroyed and blown away to the northeast. Fortunately, since no people were there, no one was hurt. In the cemetery nearby, most of the monuments were blown over. About a quarter-mile south of the church was Chris Stanley's home and barn on his farm. His place was near the southern side of the tornado as it was passing by. So his home and barn were only slightly damaged. However, about a quarter-mile north of the church where Marion and Rosa Sullivan's home was located, it was in the middle of the tornado as it went by. So their home was completely destroyed.

About a half-mile north of Marion's home and on County Road 1900E was Virgil Davenport's home and barn on his farm. Virgil's youngest sons, John and Hal, were living with his father, George

Davenport, since his wife had died a few years before. However, he still had some of his other children living with him. When his farm was hit, his home and barn were badly damaged but not completely destroyed. One of his sons who still lived with him was the only person in his home when it was hit. Since his son was in the only part of the home that was not damaged, he was not hurt at all. A home that was along County Road 1900E and about a quarter-mile farther north of Virgil's home was only slightly damaged since it was along the northern edge of the tornado as it went by.

As the tornado was roaring on across County Road 4 and was almost one-and-a-half miles wide, a lot of places were damaged or destroyed along this road. South of Highway 14 on this road, three farms were hit, and someone driving along the road had his car damaged. John Charles's home was about a half-mile south of Highway 14 and on the western side of the road. His home was near the southern edge of the tornado as it was going by, and his home was only slightly damaged. Over on the other side of the road was George Coleman's farm. The only building that the tornado damaged on his place was his barn, which was on the northern side of his farm. It was badly damaged and blown down. Farther north of George Coleman's barn along this road was George Davenport's farm.

In the early afternoon, George saw it was getting cloudy outside, and just before three o'clock, he saw that a dangerous black cloud was coming toward this area. This worried him, so he drove over to Bell School and picked up his grandsons, John and Hal Davenport, and brought them back home. After they got home and were in the house, George told his wife, Delia Ann, and their thirty-year-old daughter, Mae, that everyone needed to get out of the house and go down into the storm cellar before the storm got there. After they all got out of the house, George said they would stay outside near the storm cellar while he did some things to make it easy for them to get out of the storm cellar if the house or other things fell on top of it. Just as he got that done, the storm really looked more dangerous, and it was getting close to them. So they quickly got down into the storm cellar, and in just a few minutes, they heard the wind get really strong.

George's grandson, Hal, was really worried while he was down in the storm cellar. And while he was down there with everyone, it seemed to him like the storm cellar was trying to be lifted up out of the ground, and he could tell it was going up and down. While this was happening, his grandfather, George, tried to hold the door so it would not open, and his grandmother, Delia Ann, and Mae helped George keep it closed. A few minutes later, the tornado moved away, so Hal and everyone else were able to get up out of the storm cellar. Hal was feeling much better when he got out storm cellar and realized the storm was gone. While he was in the yard, he could see house chimney tops all over the yard. He also saw that part of the home's roof had been blown off, but it had not been destroyed. One of George's barns that was over on the other side of the road had been destroyed. Also, he saw that the chicken house on this side of the road had been demolished. However, he saw that one of George's barns near this home was not badly damaged. Hal was really glad that his grandparents' home had not been destroyed and he could get in there. Fortunately, no one there had been hurt.

A view of George Davenport's storm cellar in April of 2005 that was still standing. This was the storm cellar that George and his grandson, Hal, went into just before the 1925 tornado hit his place (Photo courtesy of Hal Davenport, and taken by Bob Johns)

Hal Davenport at his store in Crossville in April of 2005, and with his wife and friend, "Ella Walker" Brown. (Photo courtesy of Hal Davenport and Ella Brown, and taken by Bob Johns)

At the Phillipstown School, which was along County Road 4 and about a mile south of Highway 14, teacher Ed Prince decided it was getting stormy, and he had the students go home and closed the school. Then he got into his car to go home and started driving north on County Road 4. After he had just passed George Davenport's home, the tornado was about to hit him. He stopped the car on the road just north of George's place. Two men who had gotten into a ditch for safety near the road yelled at him to join them. But just after he got out of his car, the tornado had arrived. Before he got to the ditch, he was blown into the field and thrown down on the ground. Then he saw his car was rolling over toward him, and he thought it was going to hit him and kill him. Then the wind blew it in a different direction, and it rolled away from him. The car continued rolling back and forth a couple more times, but it never hit him. However, some hail hitting him was hurting him, and his face turned black and blue. After the tornado was gone, Ed walked over to where his car was and found it had been badly damaged. He could not use it to go home, so he walked home.

About an eighth of a mile north of Highway 14 and on the eastern side of County Road 4 is where John Langford's home and barn were located. As the tornado roared across his place, his home and barn were destroyed. More than a quarter-mile north of John's place and near the intersection of County Roads 4 and 1975N was John Bennett's farm and Shelley Stanley's farm. John's farm was on the western side of County Road 4, and his home was on the southern edge of County Road 1975N. As the tornado was roaring toward John's farm, his wife, Zella, and their daughter, Mary, were inside their house. John, his twenty-two-year-old son, Fred, and teenager Lawrence Watson were in his cellar sprouting potatoes. When the tornado hit his place, his home and outbuildings were destroyed. As the cellar was broke open, a sill from the home hit Fred's head and neck and killed him instantly. The same sill pinned Lawrence onto the ground, and he was hurt, but not killed. John, Zella, and Mary were either not hurt or not injured very much.

East of John's farm and on the eastern side of County Road 4 was Shelley Stanley's farm. As the tornado was roaring toward his farm, Shelley was not home, but his wife and son were. As the tornado was crossing County Road 4 on the western edge of their farm, it hit Tom Cotton's car as he was driving by, and it was blown into a ditch just off the eastern side of the road. As the car was torn up, Tom was blown away and landed in Shelley's field. The tornado also blew away all of Shelley's outbuildings and his house. The only thing left where his house had been was the concrete walk that led to where the house's front steps had been. Shelley's wife and son were seriously hurt when the house was blown away. Tom Cotton was not hurt much, and after the tornado was gone, he got up and walked over to where Shelley's house had been. He found Mrs. Shelley Stanley and her son and removed them from the wreckage. When Shelley got home, he was able to immediately get his wife and son taken over to a hospital in Evansville for treatment. By late the next day, they had recovered.

About a quarter-mile north-northeast of Shelley's home and on the eastern side of County Road 4 was Chris Hughes's home and barn on his farm. When his place was hit, his barn was completely destroyed. His house had its new rooms demolished, but the two rooms that were built probably seventy-five years before were still standing after the tornado had roared away.

On up northeast about a half-mile and on the eastern side of County Road 4 was Susan Sharp's barn and the Hughes School. When the tornado came by, Susan's barn was destroyed. Hughes School was next to the northern edge of the tornado as it was going by, and it was only slightly damaged, and no one was hurt.

As the tornado roared on east of County Road 4, it hit and destroyed Richard Hanks's home on County Road 1985N. Then it was reaching the bluff just above the Wabash River bottomland. Before it moved off the bluff and hit Louis Moser's farm, his home and barn were destroyed. His wife, Elizabeth, was at home when it was hit, and she was slightly injured. As the tornado was moving across the bluff, many of the trees up there were swept off the bluff north, east, and south of Louis's place, and they fell down into the bottomland.

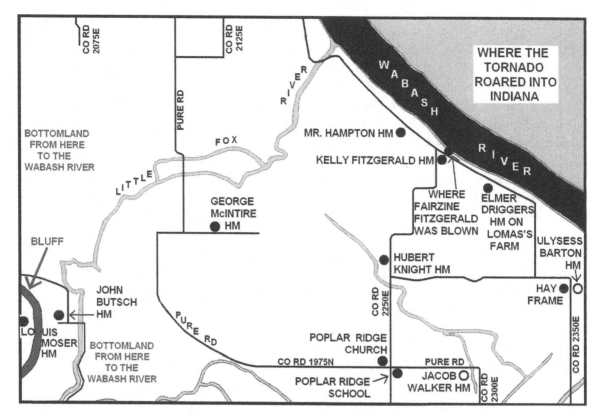

Black circle points that show damage locations in the eastern part of Phillips Township mostly in the Bottomland area near Wabash River. One black circle point shows where a lady landed after she was blown from her home. Two white circle points show where homes were not hit by the tornado and were not damaged.

As the tornado roared into the bottomland area, there were fewer homes and buildings hit. Not as many people were living there since the Wabash River occasionally flooded the bottomland area. The first place hit in the bottomland area was John Butsch's place. John's wife, Lucy, and some of their children were at home when the tornado hit his place. His home and barn were destroyed, and Lucy and some of his children were hurt.

About one mile northeast of John's place and just east of the Pure Road was where George and Edith McIntire's home was located in the bottomland. When the tornado roared across his home, it was destroyed. Down more than a mile southeast of his place and next to the intersection of Pure Road and County Road 2250E was where the Poplar Ridge Church and the Poplar Ridge School were located. Ella Walker was in the school that day, which was just on the southeastern side of the intersection. In the early afternoon, her father, Jacob Walker, who was at home, noticed when he looked out west that the weather was getting stormy. He decided to go over to the school and pick up Ella and his son, Earl, since it would not be good for them to walk home when it got stormy. After he had picked them up and took them home, Ella noticed it was starting to get stormy. After a few minutes, it started raining hard, and it was really getting dangerously windy. After a while, when it quit raining and was not dangerously windy, Ella noticed it was really getting sunny outside and the storm was over. Since her family's home was not damaged, she did not know that a tornado had just gone by north of them. However, she later found out about the tornado when a neighbor came by and told her about places north of there that had been destroyed. On the next day when Ella talked with her teacher at school, she found he was still in the school when the tornado was going by. Even though the tornado was roaring by just north of the school, some strong winds from the storm that was running the tornado blew the belfry off the school, and the teacher saw it going away from the school and dropping on the ground east of the school. Fortunately, that was the only damage that happened at the school. Also, it was found that the Poplar Ridge Church that was just on the northwestern side of the intersection had worse damage than the school since its steeple was blown off when that tornado came by, but that was the only damage that happened there anyway.

*"Ella Walker" Brown in Crossville in April of 2005. Ella and her father, Jacob Walker,
had gotten home when the 1925 tornado went by just north of them.
(Photo courtesy of Hal Davenport and Ella Brown, and taken by Bob Johns)*

More than a half-mile north of the church and school and on the western side of County Road 2250E was Hubert Knight's farm. When the tornado hit his place, his home had a part of its roof blown off, and his barn was blown away. Fortunately, no one was hurt there. After hitting his place, the tornado was roaring on toward the Wabash River and was about to move out of White County. However, several places near the western side of the river in Phillips Township were going to be hit.

On the day of the tornado, about three-and-a-half miles northeast of Crossville, the school near the town of Calvin was closing down in the afternoon. As it closed down, student Norbet Barton, and his younger brother, Cyril, got in their horse's small wagon. Norbet got the horse to start going home. They had to go more than four miles to the southeast to get to the home of their father, Ulysses Barton, which was in the bottomland close to the Wabash River. When they got about a half-mile down the road and were near John Bond's home, which was on the bluff next to the Wabash River bottomland, they saw a huge dangerous black cloud that was rotating around and was about to cross down south where they were going. Norbet stopped their horse at John's home and took Cyril off the wagon. He made him stay at John's place because he thought that many places down where they were going, including their family's home, might be destroyed. Cyril was pleased that he was staying at John's place since his friend from school, Val Wooden, lived there. Just after Norbet left with his horse, Cyril, along with Val and John's family members who were up on the bluff, watched the tornado as it roared across the bottomland about two miles south of where they were. They realized that things were being torn up since they could see shiny metal and debris of all kinds flying around in the air down there. Cyril was really worried about what might have happened to his parents down there where his home was.

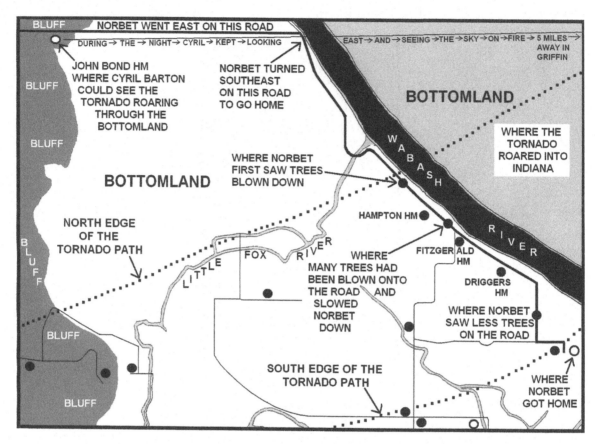

This map shows where Cyril Barton saw the tornado going by and afterwards during the night he saw fire in the sky to the east. It also shows the roads where Cyril's brother Norbet Barton went home on his horse, and three black circle points show where he saw damage on the road.

Cyril Barton standing on County Road 2350E in August of 2007. And just behind him is where his father, Ulysess Barton, had his home in 1925 when the tornado occurred. And Cyril was up north in John Bond's home and saw the tornado going by. (Photo courtesy of Cyril Barton, and taken by Bob Johns)

After Norbet left John's place, he had his horse get on the road and went down into the bottomland. Then he started going east over to the Wabash River. While he was still going east on this road, he could see the tornado that was roaring by south of him was starting to move away from the Wabash River bottomland. When he got over next to the Wabash River and had to turn southeast on another road to get home, he saw the tornado had completely moved away from the Wabash River bottomland. So he now knew that it was safe for him to go southeast on this new road along the big river so he could get to his family's home. As he was going along this road and had just crossed over the Little Fox River, he started to see that a lot of damage had occurred farther down this road, which was on the western side of the Wabash River. When he got about a quarter-mile away from the Little Fox River he crossed, he found that some trees had been blown down, and one was on the edge of the road. As he continued going on southeast along the road, there was a lot of debris and some trees on or next to the road, and he started to see places where some people's homes and buildings had been destroyed. When he had gotten almost three-quarters of a mile from where he had crossed over the Little Fox River, he found that many trees had fallen onto the road, and it was getting hard for his horse to keep going. He had his horse jump over some of the tree limbs and go around some of the root logs. It took him a long time to get through the damaged area, but when he had gotten about a half-mile away from his father's home, not many trees were on the road anymore. And when he got home, he was pleased to see that his family's home had not been damaged.

Some of the homes that were known to have been destroyed along this road that Norbet was going on next to the Wabash River were those of Mr. Hampton, Kelly Fitzgerald, and Elmer Driggers. They were the last homes hit in White County, and they were all on the western side of the road. The farthest north home along this road that was known to have been hit was Mr. Hampton's home. Old Mr. Hampton was at home when the tornado was roaring toward him. When he saw it coming, he ran outside, laid down in a ditch next to the road, and held on to a fence post. As the tornado destroyed his house, some debris fell on him, and he was injured. Fortunately, he was not badly hurt.

The farthest south home along this road that was known to have been hit was the home that Elmer Driggers had recently rented on the Lomas farm. His wife Kate's older brother, sixty-two-year-old Frederick Bodishbaugh, was in this house when the tornado was coming. When he heard the noise, he went over to the house door and held on to the doorknob. As the tornado hit the house, most of it was blown away. However, the door that Frederick was holding on to was not blown away, and he was not hurt.

Between Mr. Hampton's home and Elmer Driggers's home on this road was Kelly Fitzgerald's place where he had a home and barn. On the day of the tornado, Kelly, his wife, Fairzine, and his father-in-law were in his home. Their neighbors, Ulysses and Zadie Barton, had been shopping in Grayville in the early afternoon. When they were going back home and were about to go by Kelly and Fairzine's home, they decided to stop there for a little bit to see them since they were good friends. As they were there, it was noticed that it was starting to get stormy outside to the west. Kelly and Fairzine tried to get their friends to stay with them until the storm had gone by, but no one there at that time knew that the storm was going to be a tornado. Zadie told Kelly and Fairzine that she and her husband had to go on home since she had to take care of some young chickens that she was raising. So they went on home, about a mile on to the southeast of Kelly's place. When they got there, Ulysses put his team of horses in the barn and unharnessed them. After he got in the house with Zadie, they noticed it was getting very stormy outside. The mile-wide tornado was going by just north of his place, so his home was not damaged. However, as he was looking outside, he saw a hay frame that was over on the western side of the road get damaged and blown up in the air, and he saw it fall down in his front yard. That was the only damage he had on his place.

After Ulysses and Zadie had left Kelly Fitzgerald's place, Kelly, Fairzine, and his father-in-law noticed that the storm was getting worse and realized it was a tornado and it was going to hit their place. They were really worried about what was going to happen to them. Kelly and Fairzine got into their kitchen and stood in the doorway. They held on to each other. Kelly's father-in-law was not with them in the kitchen. When the tornado hit Kelly's place, his home and barn were completely destroyed, and Kelly knew he and Fairzine were blown away. When Kelly woke up, he had been hurt, and he was really feeling bad from his injuries. As he got up, he saw that he had been blown into a wooded area near the Wabash River, which was on the eastern side of the road and almost two-hundred yards east of where his house had been. He looked around where he was, but he could not see Fairzine or his father-in-law near the place where he landed. He walked back to where his house had been and saw it had been blown away, and he was not able to find Fairzine and his father-in-law around there either. He was really worried since he was in bad shape and had not found his family. He decided he needed someone else to help him find his family. So he started running down the road for a mile to meet with his friend, Ulysses, and see if he could help him find his family.

Down at Ulysses Barton's home, after the tornado was gone, Ulysses was sitting in the front room when he heard someone rattling on his front door. When he opened the door, he saw that it was Kelly, and he could see that blood was streaming down from his face and was all over him. He also noticed that his shirt had been torn up, and he seemed to be in very bad shape. Kelly said, "Our home was destroyed and me and Fairzine were blown away. I landed close to the river, but I don't know where Fairzine landed and I have not been able to find her or her father who lives with us. I hope I can get someone who will help me find them." Ulysses said, "I will go over there with you right now and help you find them." So they got together and went back up to Kelly's place to find Fairzine and his father-in-law. When they got up there and were near where his house had been, they saw his father-in-law. He told them that, when the tornado was coming, he went out in the yard, laid down on the ground, and held on to a clothesline post. When the tornado hit him, he was blown away, and he landed well over east next to the Wabash River. Fortunately, he was not hurt very much. But he also had not found where Fairzine was located. Because he had not found her, Kelly and Ulysses went on around the area looking for her. As they did this, they noticed some other people here were trying to find out what happened in this area. But they had not found Fairzine either. When Kelly and Ulysses went down near the river, they did find where several of Kelly's horses had been blown, and two had been killed.

It took them a long time to find Fairzine, and it was getting dark outside when they finally found her. She had been blown close to the Wabash River, like her husband and father. They saw she was been dropped on a log, and another log was lying on top of her. That was why it was hard for them to find her. Kelly ran over to get her. She was very badly hurt, and while Kelly was holding her in his arms, she died. After this had happened, some of the people who were there were able to take Kelly, his father-in-law, and his dead wife someplace away from here since they needed a place to stay.

After Fairzine was found, Ulysses started going back home. When he got there, he saw his son, Norbet, who had gotten back home quite a while ago from Calvin School. He learned that his son, Cyril, was at John Bond's place and would be staying there overnight. He was glad that they were okay and the tornado had completely left White County.

The last places destroyed in Phillips Township and White County were Kelly Fitzgerald's home and barn and the other places north and south of his place on the same road next to the Wabash River. Fairzine was the last person that the tornado killed while it was in White County. The tornado roared out of White County at 3:58 p.m., which was fairly late in the afternoon. And that is why it was getting dark when Fairzine was later found.

After the tornado had roared out of White County and got into Indiana, it did not end very soon, and it stayed very dangerous and killed a lot more people. During the night after the tornado occurred in Phillips Township, Cyril Barton, who was staying in John Bond's home, kept seeing the sky light up with fire over to the east every time he woke up. Also, John's family kept seeing that, too, when they woke up during the night, and they wondered what it was. All night long, they were seeing fire that had developed in places that the tornado destroyed in Griffin, Indiana, five miles east of John's home. The tornado killed many people there, and some were killed because the fire burned them. This was similar to how Barbara Maurer was killed in central Phillips Township.

In White County, the tornado did not hit any towns, but it caused a lot of damage in the rural areas. There were four churches, eight schools, and more than 120 homes that were damaged and destroyed, and at least twenty-nine people were known to have died because of the tornado. In Enfield Township, fifteen of the people who died were known to have died because of the tornado. They were in rural areas. A lot of damage occurred in Carmi Township, and the tornado injured a lot of people. Seven people died. The tornado just crossed a small part of Burnt Prairie Township, but it damaged and devastated at least seven homes and a church. Two people died. The tornado almost missed Hawthorne Township but destroyed a school and a home in the northwestern edge of the township. A lot of the students were injured, and one was killed. Phillips Township was a very wide township, and the tornado roared all the way across it and destroyed and damaged more than fifty homes and buildings. Four people died.

The Devastation in Franklin, Hamilton, and White Counties in Illinois from the Tristate Tornado

As the 1925 Tri-State Tornado that was about a mile-wide roared into Franklin County at 2:46 p.m. and roared out of White County at 3:58 p.m., there was a lot of devastation in Franklin, Hamilton, and White County during these seventy-two minutes. On the maps, there are 377 damaged or destroyed homes that were known where they were located. However, the actual number of homes in these three counties that were damaged or destroyed was likely more than five hundred. Most of these additional homes were likely in the town of West Frankfort. It was known where all or the churches and schools there were damaged or destroyed were located and are on the maps. Thirteen churches and twenty-three schools were known to have been damaged or destroyed in this part of Illinois. Almost 250 people were known to have died in these three Illinois counties. This was really a bad seventy-two minutes to be in this area.